**THE POLITICS
OF CORRUPTION**
Organized Crime in
an American City

THE POLITICS
OF CORRUPTION
Organized Crime in
an American City

JOHN A. GARDINER

Russell Sage Foundation
New York 1970

PUBLICATIONS OF RUSSELL SAGE FOUNDATION

Russell Sage Foundation was established in 1907 by Mrs. Russell Sage for the improvement of social and living conditions in the United States. In carrying out its purpose the Foundation conducts research under the direction of members of the staff or in close collaboration with other institutions, and supports programs designed to improve the utilization of social science knowledge. As an integral part of its operations, the Foundation from time to time publishes books or pamphlets resulting from these activities. Publication under the imprint of the Foundation does not necessarily imply agreement by the Foundation, its Trustees, or its staff with the interpretations or conclusions of the authors.

To the memory of

V. O. KEY, Jr.

who encouraged us to ask many of these questions

Acknowledgments

A research project which develops over a three-year period incurs many debts, only a few of which can be acknowledged here. The initial impetus for this study came from Lloyd Ohlin, Charles Rogovin, and Henry S. Ruth, Jr., of the President's Commission on Law Enforcement and Administration of Justice. A generous grant from the Russell Sage Foundation made it possible to expand the initial thought of a short report into an extensive study of the politics of corruption. Supplementary grants from the National Science Foundation (to the Computing Centers of the University of Wisconsin and the State University of New York at Stony Brook), the Research Committee of the University of Wisconsin, and the Research Foundation of the State University of New York financed the analysis of statistical data and the typing of the final manuscript. Professor Harry Sharp and the staff of the Wisconsin Survey Research Laboratory offered invaluable assistance in the preparation and execution of the sample survey discussed in Chapter Four, and the Roper Public Opinion Research Center at Williams College made available the results of surveys conducted in other areas.

To a large extent, the shape of this volume reflects the talents and energies of a very gifted group of graduate students at the University of Wisconsin. David and Sandra Olson shared with my family in the trials and tribulations of field research in an unfamiliar city. Keith Billingsley, Michael R. Kagay, Joel Margolis, and Bruce I. Oppenheimer designed and executed much of the statistical work in this study.

Earlier versions of this work profited from the thoughtful comments offered by Charles Cnudde, Kenneth M. Dolbeare, Charles F. Levine, Murray Edelman, Herman Goldstein, Arnold Heidenheimer, Clifford Karchmer, Michael Lipsky, Donald J. McCrone, Glenn D. Paige, Charles Raith, Howard Scarrow, James C. Scott, Ira Sharkansky, Paul Weaver, Stanton Wheeler, and James Q. Wilson.

Finally, I must express my gratitude to the people of Wincanton. The officials, employees, and organizations of the city gave freely of their time and made many suggestions which have been incorporated into this study. As with the journalists and law-enforcement officials who made available much delicate or confidential information, I respect their desires to remain anonymous.

Certain portions of this volume previously appeared in "Wincanton: The Politics of Corruption," in President's Commission on Law Enforcement and

Administration of Justice, *Task Force Report: Organized Crime* (1967), and "Public Attitudes toward Gambling and Corruption," in the November, 1967, issue of the *Annals of the American Academy of Political and Social Science*.

This research was completed before I joined the staff of the National Institute of Law Enforcement and Criminal Justice. Neither the Institute nor the United States Department of Justice necessarily supports the conclusions reached in this study.

Contents

List of Tables

chapter one

Law Enforcement, Corruption, and Urban Politics

IN THE middle of the twentieth century, organized crime has become a major force in American life. The 1967 Report of the National Crime Commission concluded that members of La Cosa Nostra can be found in many areas of the United States, and that smaller independent groups operate in many other cities. Estimates of the gross revenues to the syndicates from gambling alone run as high as $7 to $50 billion per year; net profits may run as high as $6 or $7 billion.[1] Despite the extensiveness of the syndicates, however, there is little reason to assume that illegal gambling is uniformly distributed across the nation. In some areas, nothing can be found more serious than two friends betting a dollar on the outcome of a football game or flipping a coin to see who buys the next round of drinks; in other cities, Las Vegas–style casinos cater to residents and conventioneers, and bets can be placed in every corner bar and tobacco shop. Part of these variations, of course, can be attributed to cultural differences: for religious or moral reasons, many Americans (including those who wrote the laws) find gambling to be immoral; others enjoy gambling, whether in the form of bingo, a daily bet on the numbers, or a roulette wheel or crap game in a ca-

---

[1] President's Commission on Law Enforcement and Administration of Justice, *The Challenge of Crime in a Free Society* (Washington: Government Printing Office, 1967), p. 189.

sino; a third group has no interest in gambling one way or the other, possibly satisfying gambling urges by playing bridge, golf, or the stock market.

Even among those cities in which it can safely be presumed that a sizeable number of residents would like to gamble (most middle-sized and all large cities), there are wide variations in the frequency and availability of gambling. A major source of such variations is the enforcement policy of the local police department. In some cities, wide-open horse parlors, numbers banks, and gambling casinos operate without police interference, while in other cities the gambling laws are enforced against everyone. Until a few years ago, for example, dozens of brothels and gambling joints could be found within a few blocks of the Albany, New York, city hall.[2] The Oakland, California, police department, on the other hand, has been known to raid not only commercial gambling operations but also gambling sponsored by labor unions, Catholic church bazaars, a local Lions' club, and a women's social organization.[3] It must be remembered, of course, that no amount of police harassment can eliminate *all* vestiges of commercial gambling. If bookies shift their pattern of operations frequently or decide to deal only with known customers, or if local judges demand that the police produce physical evidence or eyewitness accounts of gambling transactions, it may be impossible for the police to convict or even locate some local gamblers. As James Q. Wilson has stated the matter, "The relevant question is not 'Is there vice in this city?' but 'Given the characteristics of the community, has or has not vice been reduced to the level one would expect from intensive police activity and prevailing judicial policies?' "[4]

What conclusions should be drawn from a city in which the level of illegal gambling has *not* been reduced to this level? In some cities, a police policy of nonenforcement of gambling laws seems to be based upon a departmental judgment that the maintenance of order (the prevention of murders, muggings, juvenile delinquency, etc.) is more important than the enforcement of laws regulating traffic, prostitution, or gambling, so the police rarely "have time" for such "trivial" matters.[5] In other cities, police tolerance of widespread illegal gambling is secured through regular payoffs from crime syndicates; arrests are made only to harass gamblers who haven't paid off or to satisfy sporadic newspaper demands for a crackdown. A third group of police departments takes a halfway position, harassing commercial gamblers

---

[2] James Q. Wilson, *Varieties of Police Behavior: The Management of Law and Order in Eight Communities* (Cambridge: Harvard University Press, 1968), p. 109.
    [3] *Ibid.,* p. 107.
  . [4] *Ibid.,* p. 101.
    [5] *Ibid.,* chap. 5.

but ignoring gambling among friends or gambling sponsored by charitable organizations.[6]

These variations in the source of police decisions not to enforce gambling laws suggest that changes in police policies (e.g., beginning strict enforcement) might come about under several different sets of circumstances. In any of these cities, strict enforcement might result from the appointment of high-level police officers who choose to use their influence within the department to encourage patrolmen or vice-squad members to arrest gamblers. When the police honestly (noncorruptly) conclude that law-enforcement duties, such as worrying about gambling violations, are less important than their order-maintenance functions, widespread public demands that these priorities be changed might lead to greater enforcement activities. Where nonenforcement is based on corruption, however, it would be necessary to end the corruption before strict enforcement policies could be implemented; corruption would lead to nonenforcement even if tactical (how do we identify and convict gamblers?)[7] and motivational (how do we induce police officials and patrolmen to place a high priority on reducing the level of gambling?) problems had been solved.

The problem of corruption[8] in the law-enforcement process thus involves a number of questions concerning both law-enforcement policy-making and urban politics generally.

First, how is this kind of corruption organized? How does a crime syndicate purchase protection for its gambling activities? Are payoffs limited to a few beat patrolmen, or do high-level police officials and city-hall politicians share in the graft? Do the syndicates work with anyone who happens to be in office, or do they also attempt to have corruptible men elected or appointed to critical positions? To what extent are law-enforcement agencies such as the state police, the F.B.I., and the Internal Revenue Service involved in

---

[6] Cf. O. W. Wilson, *Police Administration,* 2nd ed. (New York: McGraw-Hill, 1963), p. 312: "The police should give their first attention to the eradication of gambling that is organized. . . . As a guide to enforcement, the seriousness of gambling violations should be judged by their extent, the amount of money involved, the open manner of the violations, and the number of participants."

[7] See G. Robert Blakey, "Aspects of the Evidence-Gathering Process in Organized Crime Cases," in President's Commission on Law Enforcement and Administration of Justice, *Task Force Report: Organized Crime* (Washington: Government Printing Office, 1967), pp. 80–113.

[8] In general, "corruption is political behavior which deviates from the formal duties of a public role because of private-regarding (personal, close family, private clique) pecuniary or status gains; or violates rules against certain types of private-regarding influence." J. S. Nye, "Corruption and Political Development: A Cost-Benefit Analysis," *American Political Science Review,* LXI (June, 1967), 419. See also Edward C. Banfield, *Political Influence: A New Theory of Urban Politics* (New York: Free Press, 1961), p. 315. A variety of interpretations and definitions of corruption are presented in Arnold J. Heidenheimer, ed., *The Analysis of Political Corruption* (forthcoming), pt. 1.

local enforcement policy-making? What role do they play in the system of corruption?

A second set of questions arising from cities with corrupt police departments concerns the relationship between the policies of the police and the values and desires of the communities they serve. Are such matters as police law-enforcement policies on gambling of active public concern, or are they peripheral to the interests of most city residents? How strong is public support for enforcement of the laws forbidding gambling and official corruption?

Third, a study of law-enforcement corruption raises a number of issues concerning the nature of urban policy-making. Who participates in the setting of police policies regarding gambling?—do the police make their own rules without substantial involvement by outsiders,[9] do they work with a few outside groups and officials particularly interested in this issue area,[10] or is a regular role played by a substantial segment of the community? Alternatively, it may be that the police enjoy a monopoly on decision-making under normal circumstances but are forced, under the pressure of unusual events, to consider outsiders' values.[11] If this last view is correct, then it is necessary to ask what kinds of events are likely to have this effect, increasing public interest in police policies and possibly producing movements for reform and strict enforcement.

A fourth set of issues concerns the consequences of corruption. Apart from the nonenforcement of state and local gambling laws, are any other aspects of city life affected? Which groups or individuals in corrupt cities, apart from the providers and consumers of gambling, incur any substantial costs or derive benefits from nonenforcement and corruption? Does corruption in the enforcement of gambling laws affect other police policies, or the activities of other city departments, or public attitudes toward their government? In short, does it make *any other* difference if the police are paid not to enforce gambling laws?

Finally, inasmuch as *widespread* corruption is an infrequent characteristic of local political systems, it must be asked whether there are certain types of social or political systems in which crime syndicates are more likely to

---

[9] Cf. J. Q. Wilson, *Varieties of Police Behavior,* p. 233: "With respect to police work—or at least its patrol functions—the prevailing political culture creates a 'zone of indifference' within which the police are free to act as they see fit." See also John A. Gardiner, *Traffic and the Police: Variations in Law-Enforcement Policy* (Cambridge: Harvard University Press, 1969), chap. 6.

[10] Cf. Wallace S. Sayre and Herbert Kaufman, *Governing New York City: Politics in the Metropolis* (New York: Russell Sage Foundation, 1960), chap. 19.

[11] Cf. the discussion of "latency" in public opinion in V. O. Key, Jr., *Public Opinion and American Democracy* (New York: Knopf, 1961), chap. 11; the concept of an "active sense of outrage," in Arnold A. Rogow and Harold D. Lasswell, *Power, Corruption, and Rectitude* (Englewood Cliffs, N.J.: Prentice-Hall, 1963), pp. 72–75; and James S. Coleman, *Community Conflict* (New York: Free Press, 1957), pp. 4–6.

succeed in capturing control of law-enforcement agencies. Are some types of social groupings, political power structures, or formal governmental arrangements (e.g., mayor-council vs. council-manager types of government) more susceptible than others to pressure from organized crime?

The following chapters attempt to answer many of these questions concerning the interrelationships among law enforcement, corruption, and urban politics. Their focus is "Wincanton," an Eastern industrial city which has been controlled by a crime syndicate for most of the last fifty years. In 1966, during a period of reform government and strict law enforcement, a team of interviewers visited the city to collect the information (including all statements not otherwise footnoted) used in the following pages.[12] Since the goal of this study is an understanding of the general phenomenon of corruption rather than an exposé of particular individuals, the names of the city and of all individuals involved have been changed.

The issues which have been outlined above will be discussed with an increasing level of abstraction and generalization. In Chapter Two, the people and politics of Wincanton will be described in order to explain the setting in which corruption developed. Chapter Three presents the basic structure of organized crime and corruption in Wincanton, emphasizing the process by which the local syndicate secured protection for its gambling activities and participated with city officials in various "free-lance" corrupt endeavors.

Beginning with Chapter Four, law-enforcement corruption will be considered as a part of other aspects of city life and politics. Chapter Four looks at public attitudes toward gambling and corruption, asking to what extent public norms regarding law enforcement and official morality were shared by the residents of Wincanton, and how such norms were distributed among the population. In Chapter Five, law-enforcement corruption will be considered as an aspect of the urban political process: after asking who is *normally* influential in law-enforcement decision-making, we will look at the conditions under which other groups (outside law-enforcement agencies, local interest groups, the voting public, etc.) become interested in police policies, and how this interest affects law enforcement and other aspects of local politics. Chapter Six discusses the impact of corruption on Wincanton—the groups and individuals who were affected by gambling and corruption, and the impact which corruption had on other governmental policies and on city politics generally. Finally, in Chapter Seven, we will ask how the probability that corruption will occur is affected by various city characteristics and how the frequency of law-enforcement corruption might be reduced.

---

[12] Copies of all interviews used in this study may be obtained from the author.

chapter two

Wincanton

FOR AT least fifty years, Wincanton has had something of a reputation as a "sin city." One worker on the staff of the National Crime Commission recalled that when he was growing up in a nearby city, Wincanton was where men went to raise hell on a Saturday night—if their wives would let them out of the house. Physically, it hardly looks the part; lacking either verdant resorts or quaint "Oldtown" or Greenwich Village charm, Wincanton looks mostly like an old, rather decayed factory town. A journalist who visited the city in 1967 summed it up as

> an almost museum piece nineteenth century industrial, immigrant-inhabited, red brick mill town. Except for a few 1930 tall business buildings, it retains exactly the look of unreconstructed 1890–1900—huddles of workers' houses nestling under overhead wires up to railroad tracks and long black factories with tall black chimneys. An Englishman from the midlands would feel perfectly at home, the abrupt descent from rich green rolling highlands and countryside to packed-in proletarian obsolescence. . . .[1]

While the physical appearance of Wincanton hasn't changed much in the twentieth century (although several upper-middle-class suburbs have grown up since World War II), a number of changes have taken place in the economic, social, and political characteristics of the city. A spurt of industrialization in the late nineteenth century transformed a rural marketplace and trading center into a bustling center for manufacturing, with a population

---

[1] Nathaniel Burt, "Report from Wincanton," *Philadelphia Magazine,* November, 1967.

exceeding 110,000 in the 1920s. Textile mills and leather-working industries dominated the local economy for many years. While the city has not known a serious depression during the last forty years (only 2.5 percent of the labor force was unemployed in 1965), it hasn't known any growth either; the central city population has been declining slowly since 1930, with a net loss of 11,000 residents between 1950 and 1960. Several textile mills and most of the leather industries have gone out of business or moved to the South, balanced somewhat by the postwar construction or expansion of machine works and electronics assembly plants.

Wincanton's postwar economy has been both diversified and dominated by national rather than locally owned corporations. The major industries today include steel processing, heavy machinery, textiles, and food products; seven corporations have more than 1,000 employees. Most of the major industries are now parts of nationwide corporations, and are operated by salaried managers rather than owner-entrepreneurs. Descendants of the original artisan-industrialists can still be found in the area, but they are primarily active in banking, investment corporations, and the law, having since the 1930s sold their stock in the family corporations.

Data from the 1960 Census show that Wincanton's population was somewhat older and had a higher proportion of lower-middle-class residents than other middle-sized cities. The Negro and Puerto Rican populations were small, and there was relatively little substandard or overcrowded housing. While there was little extreme poverty in Wincanton, there was also little great wealth within the city's boundaries. Only 11 percent had incomes over $10,000, and only 27 percent had completed high school. The vast majority of Wincanton residents belonged to the lower-middle and middle classes, with incomes between $3,000 and $10,000. There has been little in-migration to the city in recent years; 88 percent of the 1960 residents were born in this state, and more than 60 percent were living in the same homes that they had occupied in 1955. This stability has encouraged the continuation of the separate identities of the various nationality groups: the Germans, Poles, Italians, and Negroes still have their own neighborhoods, stores, restaurants, social clubs, and political leaders.

Politics in Wincanton. During the years when American cities were controlled by highly centralized political machines, it was possible for men seeking illegal privileges to control the entire city government simply by bribing the boss, who then arranged for the "cooperation" of low-level policemen, councilmen, judges, and so forth; uncooperative subordinates quickly found themselves deprived of their offices or patronage.[2] In more recent years, some city charters have given mayors a few of the powers of the old-time bosses, but nonpartisanship, the formal fragmentation of metropolitan government, civil service, the growth of unions within the municipal bureaucracy,[3] and the separate election of many city officials have meant that few mayors today are able to guarantee the acquiescence of all parts of the city government in any policy, whether legal or illegal.[4]

Where, as is often the case in American cities today, the local political system is not centralized enough to give total control to one or a few men, the next best hope for a crime syndicate seeking protection for its illegal activities is a political system which is so decentralized that *no* political force is powerful enough to challenge any individual officials who have been corrupted. For reasons that will be discussed later, such fragmented systems seem both to attract more temptable leaders and to contain fewer forces, such as party organizations, interest groups and elite associations, which might persuade tempted officials to conform to legal norms.[5]

Wincanton is an almost perfect example of such a weak, fragmented system in terms of both its formal governmental structure and its informal political processes. Many governmental functions are handled by independent boards and commissions, each able to veto proposals of the mayor and city council. The city government is a modified version of the commission plan, with a council composed of the mayor and four councilmen. In odd-numbered years, two councilmen are elected (on a partisan ballot) to four-year terms. The mayor is directly elected by the voters for a four-year term. Every two years, following local elections, the five members of the council meet to decide who will control which departments (with the statutory requirement that the mayor *must* control the police department). Thus the city's affairs can be shared equally by the five men, or a three-man majority can control most important departments. (In one not atypical occurrence, a councilman disliked by his colleagues found himself controlling only garbage collection and the Main Street comfort station!) After the biennial allocation of city departments, each department head (mayor or councilman) has fairly

---

[2] Henry Jones Ford, "Municipal Corruption," *Political Science Quarterly,* XIX (December, 1904), 673–686.

[3] Theodore J. Lowi, "Machine Politics—Old and New," *The Public Interest,* No. 9 (Fall, 1967), 83–92.

[4] For a discussion of the problems involved in aggregating political power, see Edward C. Banfield, *Political Influence: A New Theory of Urban Politics* (New York: Free Press, 1961), especially chaps. 8 and 11.

[5] A similar argument, regarding the relationship between structural centralization and corruption in labor unions, is made by Seymour Martin Lipset in *The First New Nation: The United States in Historical and Comparative Perspective,* Anchor ed. (Garden City, N.Y.: Doubleday, 1967), pp. 225–226.

strong control over the actions of his departments; while the entire council must formally ratify most personnel and budgetary matters, a "gentlemen's agreement" usually leads to council approval of the requests of department heads. Thus official decision-making in Wincanton is for all practical purposes divided into a series of "decision centers"[6] dominated by the individual city departments and the councilmen who control them; the mayor and other council members seldom intervene in departmental decisions, so there is little coordination of city activities, and councilmen can follow whatever policies are satisfactory to their bureaucracies and relevant interest groups.

Supplementing the commission structure in producing a corruptible local government in Wincanton is the limited nature of state supervision of local affairs. The state civil service laws do little to constrain official actions, since they apply only to the police, engineering, and electrical departments and building and health inspectors; within the police department, the mayor has complete authority to promote and demote officers, including the chief, although men can only be *removed* from the force "for cause."[7] Every election leads to a wholesale reorganization of the police department; patrolmen have been named chief and former chiefs have been reduced to walking a beat. As will be seen later, the state police seldom enter a city unless asked to do so, thus allowing local officials to set whatever law-enforcement policies they wish. The state's municipal bidding law also contains many loopholes inviting fraud. Cities are not required, for example, to seek competitive bids for "emergency work," "patented and manufactured materials," insurance policies, personal or professional services, or contracts involving less than $1,500. Even when bids are sought, the city is free to reject the lowest bidder where others are felt to offer superior judgment, skill, or promptness, and courts will only set aside such contracts if a complainant can *prove* that the city acted corruptly or in bad faith.

Just as these formal qualities of Wincanton government have led to a decentralization of official authority, a number of informal characteristics of Wincanton politics have also minimized the likelihood that any nongovernmental group can or will control city officials or their policies. Since the 1940s, when the Socialist Party faded from view, the Democratic Party has easily won most local elections, and there are now about two registered Democrats for each Republican in the city. Neither party organization has, however, been able to control primary elections or voting in city council

---

[6] Wallace S. Sayre and Herbert Kaufman, *Governing New York City: Politics in the Metropolis* (New York: Russell Sage Foundation, 1960), chap. 19.

[7] For an early analysis of means by which city officials can evade or manipulate civil service laws, see V. O. Key, Jr., "Methods of Evasion of Civil Service Laws," *Southwestern Social Science Quarterly*, xv (March, 1935), 337–347.

meetings. Council voting has crossed party lines as often as it has followed them. Although both party organizations have had ample patronage to dispense from state, county, and local positions, their endorsements have never guaranteed victory in the primaries. No Wincanton mayor has ever succeeded himself in office; four of the last five mayors have been defeated in bids for re-election, often unable to survive even their own party's primary. Primary election contests have seldom offered a confrontation of issue- or program-based factions; candidates tend rather to appeal to the voters on the basis of their personalities, ethnic background, or ability to deliver such favors as street improvements, playgrounds, or city jobs. Local custom requires every politician to visit the ethnic associations, ward clubs, and voluntary firemen's associations during campaign time—buying a round of drinks for all present and leaving money with the club stewards to hire poll watchers to advertise the candidates and to guard the voting booths.

No private interest groups (other than the crime syndicates) have dominated Wincanton politics in recent years. Labor unions support Democratic candidates in the general elections, but are often split in the primaries, with the industrial unions backing liberal or reform candidates and the trade unions endorsing "regulars." The unions' influence in Wincanton politics has been weakened by the fact that leaders of the local labor council have been more interested in state and national issues (minimum wage and right-to-work laws, working conditions, etc.) than in control of the city government. The newspapers, business organizations, and "good government" groups almost always support Republican candidates, but they have only been able to overcome the normal Democratic majority when monumental scandals have shaken the confidence of registered Democrats (see Chapter Five).

A number of Wincantonites interviewed in 1966 felt that even if the party organizations and unions didn't control local politicians, there was a small cabal of bankers and industrialists who "really" dominated local politics.[8] Members of this supposed elite are amused by these persistent legends, feeling that few local politicians care much about their opinions. One felt that his *father* could have called a meeting "to settle everything"—as current folklore says he and his friends are now capable of doing—but that no one

---

[8] The literature on the political activities of local elites is enormous. A useful compilation can be found in Charles Press, ed., *Main Street Politics: Policy-Making at the Local Level* (East Lansing: Michigan State University Institute for Community Development, 1962). More recent positions in this controversy include Nelson W. Polsby, *Community Power and Political Theory* (New Haven: Yale University Press, 1963); Robert R. Alford, "The Comparative Study of Urban Politics," in Leo F. Schnore, ed., *Social Science and the City: A Survey of Urban Research* (New York: Praeger, 1968); Richard M. Merelman, "On the Neo-Elitist Critique of Community Power," *American Political Science Review,* LXII (June, 1968), 451–460.

has this sort of power today.[9] Why is this elite no longer able to control Wincanton politics? For one thing, the structure of the Wincanton economy has changed: local families no longer own the major industries, and thus lack the political resource of control over jobs. Furthermore, most members of the financial-business-managerial community live in the suburbs and are ineligible to vote for or hold city office, although they contribute regularly to Republican candidates. Finally, control over local officials, if obtainable, would offer few rewards to these men; they live in beautiful suburbs which provide excellent schools, parks, playgrounds, museums, etc., so central city policies have little impact on their personal lives.

One major exception to both the political inactivity of these men and the irrelevance of city policies to them concerns the issue of economic development. As the focus of the elite has moved from the ownership of industry to the management of money, the bankers and investors have been particularly interested in the attractiveness of the Wincanton area to possible industrial developers. Since World War II, although they have been detached from policy-making in other matters, the leaders of the Wincanton business community have been quite concerned about policies related to urban redevelopment, industrial land banks, and other schemes for bringing new industry into the city. Frequently, plans for such economic growth have been developed outside the city government through urban renewal authorities, advisory panels on economic problems, and economic development corporations. This separation from the city council and electoral politics has somewhat increased the potential for elite influence, and each of these agencies has usually been dominated by members or representatives of the business and financial communities.[10]

If the elites of Wincanton have become dissociated from all political

---

[9] Changes over time in the power of urban elites are studied by Robert A. Dahl, *Who Governs?: Democracy and Power in an American City* (New Haven: Yale University Press, 1961); Robert O. Schulze, "The Role of Economic Dominants in Community Power Structure," *American Sociological Review*, XXIII (February, 1958), 3–9, and "The Bifurcation of Power in a Satellite City," in Morris Janowitz, ed., *Community Political Systems* (New York: Free Press, 1961), pp. 19–80; Robert H. Salisbury, "Urban Politics: The New Convergence of Power," *Journal of Politics*, XXVI (November, 1964), 775–797; Donald A. Clelland and William A. Form, "Economic Dominants and Community Power," *American Journal of Sociology*, LXIX (March, 1964), 511–521; David L. Westby, "The Civic Sphere in the American City," *Social Forces*, XLV (December, 1966), 161–169; Donald S. Bradley and Mayer N. Zald, "From Commercial Elites to Political Administrators: The Recruitment of the Mayors of Chicago," *American Journal of Sociology*, LXXI (September, 1965), 153–167; Ernest A. T. Barth, "Community Influence Systems: Structure and Change," *Social Forces*, XL (October, 1961), 58–63; Mayer N. Zald and Thomas A. Anderson, "Secular Trends and Historical Contingencies in the Recruitment of Mayors," *Urban Affairs Quarterly*, III (June, 1968), 53–68.

[10] See the discussion of the role of elites in urban renewal decision-making in New Haven in Dahl, *op. cit.*, chap. 10.

activities except those involving economic growth (whether this dissociation has been voluntary or involuntary is here beside the point), why should they be mentioned in this discussion of law enforcement, corruption, and organized crime? Most of the time, the inactivity of the Wincanton elites has had only a negative inpact, leaving politics and power to lower-middle-class politicians and voters; upper-middle-class attitudes toward crime and law enforcement are thus less often presented either in campaign oratory or in official deliberations. The elites have, however, maintained an interest in the *image* of the city, and have reacted indignantly when scandals have exposed the extent of corruption and organized crime in Wincanton. One manufacturer told of attending a convention in California at which he was called upon to defend not the quality of his products but the honor of Wincanton. ("You're from Wincanton?" a conventioneer is supposed to have asked. "Boy, have I heard about the hoodlums and crooked politicians you've got there!") This national image of corruption, some bankers and industrialists said, has kept potential investors from choosing Wincanton as a site for the location of new industry. Whether we attribute the elite's concern for the city's image to economic self-interest ("We must keep the city growing to find investment opportunities for our capital") or to *noblesse oblige* boosterism ("Our families made this city great and we don't want cheap politicians and crooks giving it a bad name"), Wincanton elites have been interested in corruption and law-enforcement policies, at least when they become notorious enough to give the city a bad name.

The Wincanton political system is thus fragmented, both formally and informally. Five virtually autonomous councilmen share in the management of city affairs. The mayor, while guaranteed control over the police department, has little power over the bureaucracies headed by other councilmen. The party organizations, while well provided with money and patronage, have been unable to control primary contests, council voting, or the activities of city officials. Unions, the newspapers, and business groups have been similarly unable to dominate local politics, so each candidate has been forced (and free) to develop his own constituency of neighbors, fellow ethnics, social clubs, and city workers, most of whom are only interested in his ability to deliver petty favors. The men attracted to city office have been predominantly locally oriented men with lower-middle-class backgrounds, although there has been some variation between parties. Republican candidates have usually been small businessmen of English or German ancestry; Democratic candidates have more frequently represented the Irish, Italian, and Polish neighborhoods. Recent "regular" officeholders have included two tavern owners, two accountants, a liquor salesman, and several union leaders; candidates running on *reform* Democratic slates, however, have usually been school teachers. Neither party, it will be noticed, has drawn candidates from big business or industry.

For at least the last thirty years, the Wincanton government has stressed "caretaker" policies,[11] offering a minimum of services to the public at a minimum cost rather than undertaking expensive or innovative programs to encourage community growth or the amenities of life. In 1910 a group of Wincanton businessmen commissioned a Harvard city planner to conduct a study of the city's problems. In his report the planner urged the city to build a park-like mall in the business district, to eliminate railroad grade crossings, to build parks and playgrounds, to develop circumferential highways, to eliminate pollution, and to improve housing in the city. Sixty years later the same issues are still facing the Wincanton city government. The city council debates the construction of a Main Street mall; a railroad still crosses Main Street, bringing shopping district traffic to a halt as trains grind past; the Wincanton River is unfit for swimming or fishing, polluted by industrial and municipal wastes; and an eighty-year-old school building still serves as a city hall.

While thus avoiding extensive programs to modernize the city (except where federal funds have been available), Wincanton officials have also done little to provide the most basic services. The city provides neither trash collection nor fire protection; while the city buys fire trucks and pays their drivers, fire-fighting is done entirely by volunteers. Comparison of Wincanton's general revenue and expenditure policies with those of other cities is rather difficult, in light of the impact of socio-economic variables[12] and state requirements[13] on such policies, but Table 2.1 suggests that Wincanton is taxing and spending less than other American cities with similar characteristics.[14] Furthermore, when Wincanton is compared with the other middle-

---

[11] Oliver P. Williams and Charles R. Adrian, *Four Cities: A Study in Comparative Policy Making* (Philadelphia: University of Pennsylvania Press, 1963), chap. 11.

[12] Studies of the impact of socio-economic factors on municipal revenue and expenditure policies include Robert C. Wood, *1400 Governments: The Political Economy of the New York Metropolitan Region* (Cambridge: Harvard University Press, 1961); Jeffrey K. Hadden and Edgar F. Borgatta, *American Cities: Their Social Characteristics* (Chicago: Rand McNally, 1965); and Harvey E. Brazer, *City Expenditures in the United States* (New York: National Bureau of Economic Research, 1959).

[13] For an illustration of the importance of *interstate* variations in city performance, see Brazer, *op. cit.*, pp. 46ff. State variations in the local share of state-local fiscal relationships are analyzed in Yong H. Cho, "The Effect of Local Governmental Systems on Local Policy Outcomes in the United States," *Public Administration Review*, XXVII (March, 1967), 31–38.

[14] In general, a regression equation predicts the value of a dependent variable from one or more independent variables. Knowledge of the relationship between population characteristics and taxation policies in a number of cities, for example, would permit us to predict that in a city with income level x and education level y, we should expect to find taxation level z. The R^2 column indicates the percent of the variance in the dependent variables which has been "explained" by the independent variables in the equation; an R^2 of 1.00 would mean that *all*

TABLE 2.1 *Wincanton Governmental Policies*

Policy	Variance Explained by Regression Equation (R^2)	Value Estimated by Regression Equation	Observed Value	Observed Value Divided by Estimated Value
Locally Financed Policies				
Per capita expenditures for police*	.50	$9.43	$7.95	.84
Per capita general expenditures*	.34	$72.58	$51.98	.72
Full-time city employees per 1,000 population*	.45	12.66	8.03	.63
Per capita revenues from taxes*	.58	$55.89	$34.71	.62
Per capita general revenues*	.43	$73.47	$44.95	.61
Per capita expenditures for fire protection*	.48	$9.30	$4.36	.48
Federally Financed Policies				
Public housing units per 100,000 population, 1966**	.44	800	843	1.05
Per capita expenditures for poverty programs, 1966**	.30	$435.00	$163.00	.37

Sources:
*1962 *County and City Data Book* (Washington: Government Printing Office, 1962).
**Data collected by Professors Michael Aiken and Robert R. Alford, Department of Sociology, University of Wisconsin.

sized cities in the state, Table 2.2 shows that it is tied for *last* place in the average ratio of actual (observed) policies to policies estimated from the cities' social and economic characteristics.

Why has this low-tax, low-spending policy been so pervasive? Later, the argument will be made that the city's history of corruption has diminished

---

variance has been "explained," while an R^2 of .00 would mean that *no* variance has been "explained."

Tables 2.1 and 2.2 are based upon a step-wise multiple regression analysis of eight governmental policies in 259 middle-sized (50,000 to 250,000) American cities. Twenty-six independent variables were used. As a measure of the deviation of a city from the policy value estimated by the regression equation, the observed value was divided by the estimated value. A ratio greater than 1.00 indicates that the city is doing *more* than had been estimated by the regression equation; a ratio *less* than 1.00 indicates that it is doing less. A complete statement of the independent variables used and their contribution to each regression equation is found in Appendix C. I am indebted to Ira Sharkansky, Bruce I. Oppenheimer, Richard Lochrie, and the Data Program and Library Service of the University of Wisconsin for their assistance in the preparation of this material, and to Robert R. Alford and Michael Aiken for the use of their data on American city policies.

TABLE 2.2 Comparison of Policy Deviations in Wincanton and Eleven Other Cities in the State*

City Policy

City	City Employees per 1,000 Population	Per Capita General Revenue	Per Capita Revenues from Taxes	Per Capita General Expenditures	Per Capita Expenditures for Police	Per Capita Expenditures for Fire Protection	Public Housing Units per 1,000 Population	Per Capita Expenditures on Poverty Programs	Average Rank
1	1.05	.91	.96	.88	.86	1.01	1.52	1.28	4.0
2	.69	.92	.85	.78	.94	1.05	1.53	.24	4.6
3	.68	1.07	.70	.87	.95	.76	.64	1.10	4.9
4	.72	.78	.76	.89	.73	.85	.34	1.96	5.1
5	.72	1.35	.65	1.38	1.29	.60	.32	.48	5.2
6	.78	.95	.86	1.09	.78	.74	.37	.15	5.6
7	.63	.71	.63	.74	1.05	.84	1.16	1.27	5.8
8	.66	.67	.62	.75	.94	.72	.13	.56	8.3
9	.38	.68	.50	.68	.90	.77	.30	1.67	8.4
10	.52	.63	.64	.68	.75	.33	2.90	.73	8.4
11	.40	.55	.56	.54	.74	.79	.34	1.59	9.2
Wincanton	.63	.61	.62	.72	.84	.47	.37	.39	
Wincanton's rank	(8)	11	(9)	9	8	11	(6)	10	
R^2	.45	.43	.58	.34	.50	.48	.30	.42	

*Each cell in this table shows the ratio between a city's observed policy and the policy estimated for it by the regression equation. Thus City 1 had 105 percent of the employees per 1,000 population predicted by the regression equation. A figure less than 1.00, therefore, indicates that the city's actual policy was lower than that predicted. The right-hand column indicates the average of each city's rank on the eight policies.

public trust in government and willingness to give greater power (and taxes) to city officials. At this point, it will only be noted that there have not been strong demands for official activism, possibly because the service-demanding upper-middle classes[15] do not live within city limits. City residents interviewed in 1966 overwhelmingly thought of the city government in terms of basic services; 83 percent cited public utilities, police protection, recreation, or education as the city services which were "most important" to them, and only 17 percent referred to social services or community growth. Respondents who were satisfied with the performance of the current (reform) administration based their opinions on perceptions of better provision of basic services such as law enforcement, street cleaning, or playgrounds. Those who were *unhappy* similarly referred to basic functions; "Crime is so bad that I'm afraid to go out at night"; "The streets are dirty"; "We need a playground in our neighborhood." Very few respondents evaluated the successes or failures of the city government in terms of issues of economic growth or amenities such as beautification or cultural opportunities. Given the pervasiveness of this interest in basic services, it is hardly surprising that few city politicians have offered or delivered more extensive programs. The main variation between recent administrations has been whether officials have been honest or corrupt. A few of them have been honest.

---

[15] James Q. Wilson and Edward C. Banfield, "Public-Regardingness as a Value Premise in Voting Behavior," *American Political Science Review,* LVIII (December, 1964), 876–887.

chapter three

The Stern Syndicate

SINCE the early 1930s, the story of gambling and corruption in Wincanton has centered around the activities of Irving Stern.[1] Born in Russia in 1898, Stern emigrated to the United States and settled in Wincanton in 1904. After he had worked for a few years at his family's fruitstand, Prohibition arrived and Stern became a bootlegger for Heinz Glickman, then controlling beer distribution throughout a three-state region.

[1] Portions of this chapter originally appeared in "Wincanton: The Politics of Corruption," in President's Commission on Law Enforcement and Administration of Justice, *Task Force Report: Organized Crime* (Washington: United States Government Printing Office, 1967), pp. 61–79.

As interest in organized crime has grown in recent years, sharp controversy has developed over the structure of American criminal syndicates. Donald R. Cressey, in *Theft of the Nation* (New York: Harper & Row, 1969), argues that a closely coordinated group of "families" known as La Cosa Nostra directs most gambling, narcotics, and prostitution in the United States. Gordon Hawkins, in "God and the Mafia," *The Public Interest,* No. 14 (Winter, 1969), 24–51, reviews the available evidence and finds little support for the single syndicate thesis. As the focus of this study is the impact of organized crime on Wincanton, I do not purport to resolve this dispute, although, as is noted in the text, there is little evidence that Irv Stern was taking orders from outside syndicates.

The controversy over the nature of organized crime has also engendered doubts about the validity of the evidence used in studies of crime syndicates, for few investigators, with or without subpoena powers, have gained access to syndicate members. For the record, my comments on the internal structure of the Stern syndicate are based upon information collected by Internal Revenue Service agents. Official corruption related to city purchases, sales, and protection of prostitutes, was documented in local trials. Other portions of this chapter are based on interviews with federal, state, and local law-enforcement agents, newspaper investigations, and talks with peripheral members of the Stern syndicate (corrupt elected officials and policemen). I did not talk with senior members of the Stern organization. Access to law-enforcement officials was obtained through my status in 1966 as a consultant to the National Crime Commission. In talking to others, I introduced myself as a college professor. In "Methodological Problems in the Study of Organized Crime as a Social Problem" (*Annals of the American Academy of Political and Social Science,* CCCLXXIV [November, 1967], 101–112), Donald R. Cressey outlines some of the difficulties encountered by the social scientist who attempts to reconstruct the organization of criminal syndicates from publicly available information.

Once after hijacking a shipment of illicit alcohol, Stern was ambushed and shot at by his infuriated rivals; Stern quickly identified his assailants for the police. At the ensuing trial, however, Stern was "unable" to recognize the defendants, and the outraged judge slapped a two-year perjury sentence on him. In 1933, shortly after Stern's release from prison, gang warfare led to the murder of Glickman; Stern seized control of part of his business and continued to sell untaxed liquor after the repeal of Prohibition in 1933. Stern was convicted on liquor violation charges several times in the late 1930s, and spent over one year in federal prison.

Coming out of prison around 1940, Stern announced to the world that he had reformed and was taking over the family's produce business. While Stern did in fact quit the bootlegging trade (legal competition and the zeal of federal enforcement agents was making bootlegging rather unprofitable), he turned his attention to the field of gambling, for Wincanton had developed a "wide-open" reputation, and state and local police were ignoring gamblers and prostitutes. Stern started with a numbers bank and soon added horse betting, a dice game, and slot machines to his activities. Former bootlegging friends from New York provided technical advice, and the family produce store served as a legitimate "cover." During World War II, officers from a nearby army base closed down Wincanton's brothels, but Stern was unaffected, since he had already concluded that possible profits from prostitution would not compensate for the threats which the houses posed to his gambling activities; public reprisals against prostitution might carry over to gambling, and, besides, gamblers had more public legitimacy or "status" than pimps.[2] In the course of federal investigations in 1951, it was estimated that Wincanton gambling had become an industry with gross receipts of $5 million each year; from bookmaking alone, Stern had net profits of $40,000 per week, and Klaus Braun, a rival who controlled five hundred slot machines, was collecting $75,000 to $100,000 per year.[3]

Irv Stern's activities in Wincanton collapsed abruptly in 1951 when these federal investigations brought about the election of a reform administration. (See Chapter Five.) Republican Mayor Hal Craig decided to seek what he

---

[2] Cf. Daniel Bell: "Aside from the fact that manners and morals have changed, prostitution *as an industry* doesn't pay as well as gambling. Besides, its existence threatened the tacit moral acceptance and quasi-respectability that gamblers and gambling have secured in the American way of life. It was, as any operator in the field might tell you, 'bad for business.'" See "Crime as an American Way of Life," in *The End of Ideology,* rev. ed. (New York: Free Press, 1962), p. 130.

[3] In light of Irv Stern's control over the Wincanton Police Department, it may seem strange that Klaus Braun was allowed to continue his independent slot-machine operations. The answer may be that Braun, a Gentile, had greater access to Wincanton club stewards and bartenders than did Stern. Further, as an unbelievably generous man (see Chapter Six), Braun had many friends in the city, and any attempt by Stern to drive Braun out of business would have been very bad for public relations.

termed "pearl gray purity"—tolerating isolated prostitutes, numbers writers, and bookies, but driving out all forms of *organized* crime, all activities lucrative enough to encourage bribery of Craig's police officers. Within six weeks after he took office, Craig and his district attorney had raided enough of Stern's gambling parlors and seized enough of Klaus Braun's slot machines to convince both men that their activities were over—for four years at least. The Internal Revenue Service was able to convict Braun and Stern's nephew on charges of tax evasion and send both to jail. From 1952 to 1955 it was *possible* to place a bet or find a prostitute in Wincanton, but you had to know someone to do it and no one was getting very rich in the process.

Toward the end of Craig's administration, it was apparent to everyone that reform sentiment was dead and that the Democrats would soon be back in office. In the summer of 1955, Stern met with representatives of several East Coast "families" of the Cosa Nostra or "Mafia,"[4] and arranged for the rebuilding of his gambling empire. His experience during the 1940s and his brush with the Internal Revenue Service, however, suggested that a number of organizational changes were in order. Stern decided to consolidate *all* Wincanton vice and gambling under his leadership, but he also decided to turn the actual operation of most activities over to others. From 1956 until the next wave of reform swept Wincanton in 1964, Irv Stern generally succeeded in attaining these goals.

The Structure of the Stern Syndicate. The financial keystone of Stern's gambling empire was numbers betting. Records seized by the Internal Revenue Service in 1959 and 1960 indicated that Stern's gross receipts from the numbers business amounted to more than $100,000 per month, or about $1.3 million annually. Since the numbers are predominantly a poor man's form of gambling (bets range from a quarter to a dollar or more), and since payoffs are made daily, a large number of writers and very tight organization are required. Effective control demands that a maximum possible number of men be on the streets contacting bettors, that the writers report their bets honestly, and finally that no one man, if arrested, is able to identify others in the organization. During the "pearl gray purity" of Hal Craig, numbers betting was completely disorganized—isolated writers wrote bets for their friends but frequently had to renege if a popular number won; no individual was strong enough to insure against such eventualities. When reform ended in 1955, however, Stern's lieutenants notified each numbers writer in Wincanton that he was now working for Stern—or else. Those

---

[4] For an analysis of the organization and activities of the criminal syndicates affiliated with the Cosa Nostra, see Cressey, *Theft of the Nation.*

who objected were "persuaded" by Stern's men or else arrested by the police, as were any writers suspected of underreporting their receipts. Few held out for very long.

After Stern completed the reorganization of the numbers business, its structure was roughly this: Eleven sub-banks (each employing from five to thirty writers) reported daily to Stern's central accounting office (which was moved periodically to evade federal enforcement agents). Thirty-five percent of the gross receipts were kept by the writers. After deducting winnings and expenses (primarily protection payoffs to the police and other officials), Stern divided the net profits equally with the operators of the sub-banks, covering winnings whenever a popular number "broke" one of the smaller operators.

During the years after 1955, Irv Stern handled prostitution and several forms of gambling on a "franchise" basis. He took no part in the conduct of these businesses and received no share of the profits, but exacted a fee for protection from the police. Several horse-betting rooms, for example, operated regularly; the largest of these paid Stern $600 per week. While slot machines had permanently disappeared from the Wincanton scene after the 1951 federal investigations, a number of men began to distribute pinball machines which gave cash prizes to players. As was the case with numbers writers, these pinball distributors had been unorganized during the Craig administration. When Democratic Mayor Gene Donnelly succeeded Craig, he immediately announced that all pinball machines were illegal and would be confiscated by the police.[5] A Stern agent then contacted the pinball distributors and notified them that if they employed Dave Feinman (Irv Stern's nephew) as a "public relations consultant," there would be no interference from the police. Several rebellious distributors formed an Alsace County Amusement Operators Association, only to see Feinman appear with two thugs from New York; after the Association president was roughed up, all resistance collapsed, and Feinman collected more than $2,000 each week to promote the "public relations" of the distributors. (Stern, however, was never able to buy protection against *federal* action; after the Internal Revenue Service began seizing the pinball machines in 1956, the owners were forced to purchase the $250 federal gambling stamps for each machine as well as paying Feinman. Over two hundred Wincanton machines bore these stamps in 1961, and thus were immune from federal action.)

---

[5] For illustrations of syndicate use of the police to destroy competitors, see Cressey, *Theft of the Nation*, chap. 9; V. O. Key, Jr., "Police Graft," *American Journal of Sociology*, XL (March, 1935), 624–636; and William F. Whyte, *Street Corner Society* (Chicago: University of Chicago Press, 1943).

While maintaining direct control of Wincanton numbers betting, and an indirect interest in horse betting and pinball machines, Stern shared with two out-of-state syndicates in the operation and profits of two enterprises, a large dice game and the largest distillery found by the Treasury Department in the East since Prohibition. The dice game employed over fifty men—drivers to "lug" players into Wincanton from as far as a hundred miles away, doormen to check players' identities, loan sharks who "faded" the losers, croupiers, food servers, guards, etc. The 1960 payroll for these men was over $350,000. Irv Stern divided the game's profits with his out-of-state partners and received an extra $1,000 per week to secure protection from the police. While no estimate of the total gross receipts from this game is available, some indication can be found in the fact that $50,000 was found on the tables and in the safe when F.B.I. agents raided the game in 1962. Over one hundred players were arrested during the raid; one businessman had lost over $75,000 at the tables.

Similar profit-sharing arrangements governed the operation of a distillery erected in an old warehouse on the banks of the Wincanton River. Stern arranged for a city permit to link the still with the city's water and sewer systems, and provided protection from local police after it went into operation. With $200,000 in equipment, the still was capable of producing four million dollars' worth of alcohol annually, and served a five-state area until Treasury Department agents raided it after it had been in operation for less than one year.

The dice game and the distillery raise questions concerning the status of Irv Stern's Wincanton organization vis-à-vis the out-of-state syndicates. Newspapers and Republican politicians in Wincanton frequently claimed that Stern was simply the local agent of the Cosa Nostra. Apart from the fact that Stern, being Jewish, was ineligible for membership in the Sicilian-dominated Cosa Nostra, the evidence suggests that Stern was far more than an agent for outsiders, even though he was regularly sending money to them. It would be more accurate to regard these payments as profit-sharing with co-investors and as charges for services rendered.[6] The East-Coasters provided technical services in the operation of the dice game and still, and "enforce-

---

[6] Just as we must wonder why Irv Stern did not close down Klaus Braun's slot-machine activities, the question arises why the East Coast families of the Cosa Nostra did not attempt to take over Irv Stern's organization. Donald R. Cressey, in a private communication to the author, suggests three possibilities. First, Stern may have been allowed to remain independent as a reward for his services to the outsiders during Prohibition. Second, he may have been regarded as the only man who could arrange for official toleration of their Wincanton dice game and still. Third, they may have concluded that he was more valuable active than inactive (or alive than dead); his operations were, after all, yielding a tidy profit to the outsiders in layoff and "enforcement" fees. A fourth possibility, equally untestable, would be that the East Coast syndicates lacked the muscle or resources to destroy Stern even if they wanted to.

ment" services for the Wincanton gambling operation. When deviants had to be persuaded to accept Stern domination, Stern called upon outsiders for "muscle"—strong-arm men who could not be traced by local police if the victim chose to protest. In 1941, for example, Stern asked for help in destroying a competing dice game; six gunmen came in and held it up, robbing and terrifying the players. While a few murders took place in the struggle for supremacy in the 1930s and 1940s, only a few people were roughed up in the 1950s and no one was killed.

After Mayor Craig's reform era ended in 1956, Irv Stern was able to establish a centralized system in which he alone determined which rackets would operate[7] and who would be allowed to operate them. How did he keep order within this system? Basically, three control techniques were operative —as a business matter, Stern controlled access to several very lucrative operations, and could quickly deprive an uncooperative gambler or numbers writer of his source of income. Second, since he controlled the police department, he could arrest any gamblers or bookies who were not paying tribute. (Some of the gambling and prostitution arrests which took place during the Stern era served another purpose—to placate newspaper demands for a crackdown. As one police chief from this era phrased it, "Hollywood should have given us an Oscar for some of our performances when we had to pull a phony raid to keep the papers happy.") Finally, if the mechanisms of fear of financial loss and fear of arrest failed to command obedience, Stern was always able to keep alive a fear of physical violence. As has been seen, numbers writers, pinball distributors, and competing gamblers were brought into line after outside enforcers put in an appearance, and Stern's regular collection agent, a local tough who had been convicted of murder in the 1940s, was a constant reminder of the virtues of cooperation. Several witnesses who had told grand juries or federal agents of extortion attempts by Stern received visits from Stern enforcers and tended to "forget" when called to testify against the boss.

The Process of Corruption. To continue to operate his various gambling enterprises, Irv Stern needed to be sure that law-enforcement agencies were immobilized. To this end, Stern worked to put cooperative men in office, to buy off those who occupied strategic enforcement positions, and to implicate

---

[7] Curiously, Stern never allowed narcotics to be sold (at least on a regular basis) while he controlled Wincanton. Explanations for this phenomenon are varied. Some Wincantonites feel that Stern had a healthy respect for federal narcotics agents. Close friends of Stern felt that the decision more likely came from a personal distaste for drugs and their users. There was also little evidence that Stern engaged in loan sharking, another lucrative activity favored by many crime syndicates, apart from one shark who catered to participants in the dice game.

most city officials in various forms of corruption so completely that they would be unable to turn upon him. Just as businessmen facing restrictions on their rates or operating practices will seek to control the choice of men who will serve on regulatory boards or commissions,[8] so Irv Stern was interested in the men who would set law-enforcement policy in Wincanton. To gain access to those *elected* officials involved with enforcement agencies, Stern early became active (if secretly) in Wincanton politics. It was noted in Chapter Two that most Wincanton election contests are decided in the Democratic primaries, and that endorsements from organizations are usually less important than support from ethnic and neighborhood blocs. Candidates devote much of their campaign time to visiting clubs and ward bars, buying drinks for all present (an expensive proposition if the visit has been well advertised), and leaving funds with the bartender or club steward to secure a good turnout of voters and poll-watchers on election day.

Success in this kind of electioneering requires either an exceptionally well known name or endorsements from most of the organizations with Democratic members—or a lot of money. No reliable figures are available (state campaign expense reporting laws are weak), but expenses for Wincanton primary candidates probably average around $5,000; the general election costs another $10,000 per man. In the chaos of the primaries, with three to five men seeking the mayoral nomination, and five or ten vying for the two seats on the council, few candidates can line up big legitimate money for media advertising or visits to the clubs. Knowing this well, Irv Stern often helped out men he felt would be tolerant if elected. In some years, he helped several candidates, not caring who won but wanting to guarantee access to all. In other years, when one candidate was particularly promising (or another particularly threatening), Stern concentrated his financial support on one man. A strange turnabout occurred in 1959, when Stern is alleged to have supported incumbent Mayor Donnelly in the primaries and asked challenging Councilman Walasek to withdraw; Walasek refused and went on to win the primary nomination. Never one to bear grudges, Stern is reported to have aided Walasek in defeating the Republican nominee in the general election.[9]

Contributions during primary and general election campaigns gave Irv Stern access to many city officials; initial contact with others came later. Following Walasek's victory in 1959, for example, the question arose as to who

---

[8] See Marver Bernstein, *Regulating Business by Independent Commissions* (Princeton: Princeton University Press, 1955).

[9] For a general discussion of the role of underworld money in American elections, see Alexander Heard, *The Costs of Democracy: Financing American Political Campaigns,* abridged ed. (Garden City, N.Y.: Doubleday, 1960), pp. 135–147.

would be named to top positions in the police department. Dave Phillips later told federal investigators that Stern's agents asked if he would be interested in the job; when he said that he was, Phillips was told that he would have to pay Stern $5,000 and that another $5,000 would be needed to give X a high position in the police department. Both men, of course, more than recouped their "investment" through payoffs from Stern and others protected by the police.

After insuring, during campaigns or otherwise, that accommodating men were in control of City Hall and the police department, Stern was careful to reward them regularly. Two basic strategies were used—to pay top personnel as much as necessary to keep them happy (and quiet), and to pay *something* to as many as possible, thus implicating them in the system and keeping them from talking. The range of payoffs thus went from a weekly salary for the mayor to liquor and a Christmas turkey for many patrolmen. Records seized in a raid on the central numbers bank indicated payments totaling $2,400 each week to the mayor, police chief, and other city and county officials.

While the list of persons to be paid remained fairly constant, the amounts paid varied according to the gambling activities in operation at the time. While the dice game was running, the mayor was reportedly receiving $1,500 per week, the chief $100, and a few policemen lesser amounts. Payoffs were cut by 50 percent when the still and dice game were driven out of business.

While the number of officials receiving regular "salary" payoffs was quite restricted (only fifteen names were on the "payroll" found at the numbers bank), many other officials were paid off in different ways. Federal investigators found that Stern had given "mortgage loans" to a police lieutenant and a police chief's son. A judge recalled that shortly after being elected, he received a call from Dave Feinman, Stern's nephew. "Congratulations, judge. When do you think you and your wife would like a vacation in Florida?" "Florida? Why on earth would I want to go there?" "But all the other judges and the guys in City Hall—Irv takes them all to Florida whenever they want to get away." "Thanks anyway, but I'm not interested." "Well, how about a mink coat instead. What size coat does your wife wear? . . ." An assistant district attorney told of seeing Feinman walking up to his front door with a large basket from Stern's supermarket just before Christmas. "My minister suggested a needy family that could use the food," he recalled, "but I returned the liquor. How could I ask a minister if he knew someone that could use three bottles of Scotch?" (Some men were also silenced free of charge to Stern—low-ranking policemen, for example, kept quiet after they learned that men who reported gambling or prostitution were ignored or transferred to the midnight shift; they didn't have to be paid.)[10]

Campaign contributions, regular payments to higher officials, holiday and birthday gifts—these were the bases of the system by which Irv Stern bought protection from the law. The campaign contributions usually ensured that tolerant officials were elected; regular payoffs usually kept their loyalty. In a number of ways, Stern was also able to enrich corrupt officials at no financial cost to himself. Just as the officials, being in control of the instruments of law enforcement, were able to facilitate Stern's gambling enterprises, so Stern, in control of a network of men operating outside the law, was able to facilitate the officials' "free-lance" corrupt enterprises. As will be seen shortly, some local officials were not satisfied with their legal salaries from the city and their illegal salaries from Stern, and decided to demand payments from prostitutes, kickbacks from salesmen, etc. Stern, while seldom receiving any money from these transactions, became a broker, bringing politicians into contact with salesmen, merchants, and lawyers willing to offer bribes to get city business, setting up "middlemen" who could handle the money without jeopardizing the officials' reputations, and providing enforcers who could bring delinquents into line.

From the corrupt activities of Wincanton officials, Irv Stern received little, at least in comparison with the profits of his gambling operations. Why then did he get involved in them? From Stern's point of view, the major virtue of the system of official extortion that flourished in Wincanton was that it kept down the officials' demands for payoffs directly from Stern. If a councilman was able to pick up $1,000 on a purchase of city equipment, he might demand a lower payment for the protection of gambling. Furthermore, since Stern knew the facts in each instance of extortion, the officials would be further implicated in the system, and thus less able to back out on the arrangements regarding gambling. Finally, as Stern discovered to his chagrin, it became necessary to supervise extortion to save officials from their own stupidity. Mayor Gene Donnelly was reported to have been cooperative, and remained satisfied with his regular "salary." Bob Walasek, who succeeded Donnelly, was more greedy, and seized many opportunities to profit from a city contract. Soon Stern found himself supervising many of Walasek's deals to keep the mayor from blowing the whole arrangement wide open. When Walasek tried to double the "take" on a purchase of parking meters, Stern

---

[10] Studies of corruption in other cities suggest that when high-ranking police officials are on the syndicate's payroll, low-level policemen are likely to feel free to enter into free-lance shakedowns, demanding or accepting bribes from motorists, merchants, and others, secure in the knowledge that their superiors are in no position to complain.

had to step in and set the contract price, provide an untraceable middleman, and see the deal through to completion. "I told Irv," Police Chief Phillips later testified, "that Walasek wanted $12 on each meter instead of the $6 we got on the last meter deal. He became furious. He said Walasek is going to fool around and wind up in jail. You come and see me. I'll tell Walasek what he's going to buy!"

The Extent of Corruption. Optimal protection for an extensive gambling operation requires control over many parts of local government. How successful was Stern? How many officials were under his control? How strong was that control? With the exception of the local Congressman and the city treasurer, it seems that a few officials at each level (city, county, and state) were involved either with Stern or with some form of free-lance corruption. Within the city administration, the evidence is fairly clear that several mayors and councilmen received regular payments from Stern and divided kickbacks on city purchases and sales. Key subcouncil personnel frequently shared in payoffs affecting their particular departments—the police chief shared in the gambling and prostitution payoffs and received $300 of the $10,500 kickback on parking-meter purchases. The councilman controlling one department may have received a higher percentage of kickbacks related to its operations than the other councilmen.

The fact that Stern had contacts in so many city departments does not, however, mean that all city employees were corrupt or that Stern had absolute control over those he supported. Both official investigations and private research lead to the conclusion that there is no reason whatsoever to question the honesty of the vast majority of the employees of the City of Wincanton. Certainly no more than ten of the 155 members of the Wincanton police force were on Irv Stern's payroll (although many of them accepted petty Christmas presents—turkeys or liquor). In each department, there were a few employees who objected actively to the misdeeds of their superiors, and the only charge which can justly be leveled against the mass of employees is that they were unwilling to jeopardize their positions by publicly exposing what was going on. When federal investigators showed that an honest (and possibly successful) attempt was being made to expose Stern-Walasek corruption, a number of city employees cooperated with the grand jury in aggregating evidence which could be used to convict the corrupt officials. Before these federal investigations began, however, it could reasonably appear to an individual employee that the entire machinery of law enforcement in the city was controlled by Stern, Walasek, *et al.*, and that an individual protest would be silenced quickly. This dilemma was documented in the momentary crusade conducted by Assistant District Attorney Phil Roper. When the district attorney left for a short vacation, Roper decided to act against local gamblers and prostitutes. With the help of the state police (who were astonished that *any* Wincanton official would be interested in a crackdown), Roper raided several large brothels. Apprehending on the street the city's largest distributor of punchboards and lotteries, Roper effected a citizen's arrest and drove him to police headquarters for proper detention and questioning. "I'm sorry, Mr. Roper," said the desk sergeant. "We're under orders not to arrest persons brought in by you." Roper was forced to call upon the state police for aid in confining the gambler. When the district attorney returned from his vacation, he quickly fired Roper for "introducing politics into the district attorney's office."

Just as the number of city employees corrupted by Stern was limited, so it must also be noted that several men who generally cooperated with Stern rebelled when his demands or external pressure became too great. One judge hated prostitutes and ordered city officials to close down several brothels protected by Stern; later, he asked for a state investigation of Stern's gambling activities after federal agents raided several bookies. Police Chief Phillips also changed his mind during his four years in office. After two years of ignoring gamblers and prostitutes, Phillips became frightened by increased federal interest in Wincanton and closed down Stern's horse-betting rooms. Finally, after a federal grand jury brought a perjury indictment against him, Phillips agreed to work for the federal government, secretly recording conversations with Stern and Walasek and testifying against them in subsequent trials.

Free-Lance Corruption. During most of the period after Prohibition, Wincanton officials tolerated Irv Stern's gambling activities. Much of the corruption in Wincanton, however, had little to do with Stern or gambling. Law books speak of at least three varieties of official corruption: nonfeasance ("failing to perform a required duty at all"), malfeasance ("the commission of some act which is positively unlawful"), and misfeasance ("the improper performance of some act which a man may properly do"). During the years in which Irv Stern was running his gambling operations, Wincanton officials were guilty of all of these. Some residents say that corrupt mayors came to regard their office as a brokerage, levying a tariff on every item that came across their desk; sometimes a request for simple municipal services turned into a game of cat and mouse, with the mayor sitting on the request, waiting to see how much would be offered, and the petitioner waiting to see if he could obtain his rights without having to pay for them. This kind of corruption was not as lucrative an enterprise as protecting gambling, but it offered a tempting supplement to low official salaries.

The most frequent form of corruption by Wincanton officials was the non-enforcement of the state's gambling laws against Irv Stern's men. Not all nonenforcement, of course, should be interpreted as corruption; police in many cities ignore violations of minor laws regarding traffic offenses, loitering, fornication, sales on Sunday, etc. In some cases, police inaction has been based on limited enforcement resources; in others, the police simply feel that no one in the community *wants* these laws enforced.[11] Most instances of nonfeasance in Wincanton, however, were clearly based on bribery or extortion. A burlesque theater manager, under attack from high school teachers for his lurid advertising, was ordered to pay $25 per week to keep his "all-the-way" strip show open. All prostitutes were tolerated who kept up their protection payments. One madame who controlled more than twenty girls made protection payments of $500 per week. Another prostitute complained to a magistrate that she not only had to pay a city official $100 per week but also that "he had a couch in his office where we had to pay again."

If nonfeasance is the failure to do something you are required to do, malfeasance is the commission of an act you are forbidden to do. City and police officials regularly fixed traffic and parking tickets, at times for money, at times as political favors. One young Puerto Rican interviewed in 1966 told of being harassed by a patrolman for parking his car on the street at night; a quiet payment of $40 to a magistrate ended the harassment. Although state law offers no clear standards by which the mayor should make promotions within his police department, it was obviously improper for Mayor Walasek to name Dave Phillips as police chief on the basis of his payment of $5,000 to Stern. Decisions based on "political contributions," however, pose a serious legal and analytical problem in classifying the malfeasance of Wincanton officials, and indeed of politicians in many cities. Political campaigns cost money, citizens have a right to support the candidates of their choice, and officials have a right to appoint their backers to noncivil-service positions. At some point, however, threats or oppression convert legitimate requests for political contributions into extortion. Shortly after taking office in 1956, Mayor Gene Donnelly notified city hall employees that they would be expected "voluntarily" to contribute 2 percent of their salary to the Democratic Party. (It might be noted that Donnelly never forwarded any of these "polit-

---

[11] See, generally, John A. Gardiner, *Traffic and the Police: Variations in Law-Enforcement Policy* (Cambridge: Harvard University Press, 1969); and James Q. Wilson, *Varieties of Police Behavior: The Management of Law and Order in Eight Communities* (Cambridge: Harvard University Press, 1968).

ical contributions" to the party treasurer.) A number of salesmen doing business with the city were notified that companies which had supported the party would receive favored treatment; Donnelly notified one salesman that in light of a proposed $81,000 contract for the purchase of fire engines, a "political contribution" of $2,000 might not be inappropriate. While neither the city hall employees nor the salesman had "rights" to their positions or their contracts, the "voluntary" quality of their contributions seems questionable.

One final example of malfeasance came in 1956 with Mayor Donnelly's abortive "War on the Press." Following a series of gambling raids by the Internal Revenue Service, the newspapers began asking why the local police had not participated in the raids. The mayor lost his temper and threw a reporter in jail, policemen were instructed to harass newspaper delivery trucks, and seventy-three tickets were written over a forty-eight-hour period for supposed parking and traffic violations. Donnelly soon backed down after national news services picked up the story and made him look ridiculous. Charges against the reporter were dropped, and the newspapers continued to expose gambling and corruption.

Misfeasance in office, says the common law, is the improper performance of some act which a man may properly do. City officials must buy and sell equipment, contract for services, and allocate licenses, privileges, etc. These actions can be said to be improperly performed either if the results are improper (e.g., if a building inspector were to approve a home with defective wiring, or a zoning board authorized a variance which had no justification in terms of land usage) or if a proper result is achieved by improper procedures (e.g., if the city purchased an acceptable automobile in consideration of a bribe paid to the purchasing agent). In the latter case, an improper result can usually be assumed as well—while the automobile will be satisfactory, the bribe-giver will probably have inflated the sale price to cover the costs of the bribe.

Given the previously noted permissive quality of the state's municipal bidding laws, it was relatively easy for council members to justify or disguise contracts in fact based upon bribes. The exemption for patented products facilitated bribe-taking in the purchase of two emergency trucks for the police department (with a $500 "campaign contribution" on a $7,500 deal), three fire engines ($2,000 was allegedly paid on an $81,000 contract), and 1,500 parking meters (involving payments of $10,500 plus an $880 clock for Mayor Walasek's home). Similar fees were allegedly exacted in connection with the purchase of a city fire-alarm system and police uniforms and firearms.

When contracts involved services to the city, the provisions in the state law regarding "the lowest *responsible* bidder" and excluding "professional services" from competitive bidding provided convenient loopholes. One internationally known engineering firm refused to agree to a kickback in order to secure a contract to design a $4.5-million sewage disposal plant for the city; a local firm was then appointed which paid $10,700 of its $225,000 fee to an associate of Irv Stern and Mayor Donnelly as a "finder's fee." Since the state law also excludes public works maintenance contracts from the competitive bidding requirements, most city paving and street-repair contracts during the Donnelly-Walasek era were given to a contributor to the Democratic party. Finally, the franchise for towing illegally parked cars and cars involved in accidents was awarded to two garages which were then required to kick back one dollar for each car towed.

The handling of graft on the towing contracts illustrates the way in which minor violence and the "lowest responsible bidder" clause could be used to keep bribe-payers in line. After federal investigators began to look into Wincanton corruption, the owner of one of the garages with a towing franchise testified before the grand jury. Mayor Walasek immediately withdrew his franchise, citing "health violations" at the garage. The garageman was also "encouraged" not to testify by a series of "accidents"—wheels fell off tow-trucks on the highway, steering cables were cut, and so forth. Newspaper satirization of the "health violations" charge forced the restoration of the towing franchise, and the "accidents" ceased. One final area of city powers abused by Walasek *et al.* covered discretionary acts such as granting permits and allowing zoning variances. On taking office, one man took control of the bureaus of building and plumbing inspection. With this power to approve or deny building permits, he "sat on" applications, waiting until the petitioner "contributed" $50 or $75 or threatened to sue to obtain his permit. Some building designs were not approved until a favored architect was retained as a "consultant." (It is not known whether this involved kickbacks or simply patronage for a friend.)

All of the activities detailed thus far involved fairly clear violations of the law. A brief discussion of "honest graft" will complete the picture of the abuse of office by Wincanton officials. This term was best defined by one of its earlier practitioners, New York State Senator George Washington Plunkitt, who loyally served Tammany Hall at the turn of the century.

There's all the difference in the world between [honest and dishonest graft]. Yes, many of our men have grown rich in politics. I have myself. I've made a big fortune out of the game, and I'm gettin' richer every day, but I've not gone in for dishonest graft—blackmailin' gamblers, saloonkeepers, disorderly people, etc.—and neither has any of the men who have made big fortunes in politics.

There's an honest graft, and I'm an example of how it works. I might sum up the whole thing by sayin': "I seen my opportunities and I took 'em."

Let me explain by examples. My party's in power in the city, and it's goin' to undertake a lot of public improvements. Well, I'm tipped off, say, that they're going to lay out a new park at a certain place.

I see my opportunity and I take it. I go to that place and I buy up all the land I can in the neighborhood. Then the board of this or that makes its plan public, and there is a rush to get my land, which nobody cared particular for before.

Ain't it perfectly honest to charge a good price and make a profit on my investment and foresight? Of course, it is. Well, that's honest graft.[12]

While there was little in the way of land purchasing—either honest or dishonest—going on in Wincanton during this period, several officials who carried on their own businesses while in office were able to pick up some "honest graft." Police Chief Phillips' construction firm received a contract to remodel the largest brothel in town. A councilman's company received a contract to construct all gasoline stations built in the city by a major petroleum company; some critics have concluded that the contract was the *quid pro quo* for the councilman's vote to award this company the city's gasoline contract.

Conclusions. It was noted in Chapter One that a police policy of not enforcing gambling laws may sometimes arise from a feeling that the maintenance of public order (preventing murder, muggings, etc.) is a task which consumes all available police resources; no one "has time," in other words, to worry about enforcing gambling, prostitution, or traffic laws. In Wincanton, the nonenforcement of gambling laws was instead based upon systematic corruption of public officials. The Stern syndicate both financed the election campaigns of tolerant candidates and made regular payoffs to city officials and senior police officers. Officials added to their syndicate payoffs by demanding bribes from individuals and companies doing business with the city or seeking legitimate city services. The result was not only the violation of many city and state laws but also the immobilization of the local law-enforcement apparatus. Reform, as will be seen in Chapter Five, only came about when *outside* law-enforcement agencies destroyed the Stern syndicate and publicized its dealings with city officials.

---

[12] William L. Riordan, *Plunkitt of Tammany Hall* (New York: E. P. Dutton, 1963), p. 3.

chapter four

Public Attitudes Toward
Law Enforcement

THE phenomenon of systematic nonenforcement of criminal laws due to official corruption raises a number of questions about the process by which public policies are made.[1] On the one hand, public policies might be viewed as manifestations of the expressed or latent values of community residents, or at least of those who are politically active; nonenforcement might thus reflect community hostility to the official laws. An alternative interpretation might be that local residents know little or nothing about the policies being followed by official agencies; a policy of nonenforcement could therefore arise through the secret machinations of corrupt officials while residents assumed that strict enforcement was being practiced.

Underlying these two views are conflicting assumptions about the direction of public attitudes toward law-enforcement policy and the importance of such attitudes in policy-making. With regard to the direction of public attitudes, one might ask whether there is strong support for antigambling legislation, open hostility, or some mixture of the two?[2] With regard to the impor-

---

[1] Portions of this chapter originally appeared in "Public Attitudes toward Gambling and Corruption," *Annals of the American Academy of Political and Social Science,* CCCLXXIV (November, 1967), 123–134.

Michael R. Kagay, Joel Margolis, and Bruce I. Oppenheimer, of the Department of Political Science, University of Wisconsin, planned and executed much of the statistical analysis used in this chapter.

[2] See, for example, Arnold A. Rogow and Harold D. Lasswell, *Power, Corruption, and Rectitude* (Englewood Cliffs, N.J.: Prentice-Hall, 1963), p. 79:

"In American cities, . . . the cycle [between corruption and reform] reflects an accommodation of conflicting and complementary interests, among 'rich' and 'poor' wards. The poor wards

tance of these attitudes (regardless of direction), do local residents know what their police are doing? Do they communicate their wishes to policy-makers? A number of recent studies have concluded that few citizens know what policies (e.g., strict or lax enforcement) are being followed;[3] the law-enforcement "decision center,"[4] rather than acting upon pressures from a wide segment of the community, usually considers only the values of the governmental agencies charged with setting and implementing law-enforcement policies, the groups and individuals who have a particular interest in enforcement issues, and (at times) the criminals whose conduct is (or is not) to be regulated.[5] Thus, unless some unusual event publicizes the policies followed by enforcement agencies and makes them particularly salient to the mass public,[6] the attitudes of the average citizen may not be particularly relevant to the process of law-enforcement policy-making.[7]

---

include high-mobility, lodging-house districts where run-down property, which is often held for speculative purposes, usually obtains highest return when used for 'immoral' purposes, especially organized prostitution and gambling. Moral standards are usually the proclaimed standards of the wealthier residential wards and of the neighborhoods abounding in children, schools and churches. The conflicting interests in law enforcement and evasion are territorially accommodated; that is 'rackets' are resisted when they spread into 'respectable' areas. The persistent pursuit of larger markets by those engaged in illegal activities, plus the chronic pressure against efficiency that results from demands for jobs and favors, tend to tip the local equilibrium against law enforcement and toward inefficiency. The resulting deprivations provoke reform crusades to restore higher levels of law enforcement, economy, and efficiency." See also Charles E. Merriam, *Chicago: A More Intimate View of Urban Politics* (New York: Macmillan, 1929), pp. 54–60; Virgil W. Peterson, "Obstacles to Enforcement of Gambling Laws," *Annals of the American Academy of Political and Social Science,* CCLXIX (May, 1950), 9–20.

  [3] For a discussion of the "low visibility" of law-enforcement policies, see Joseph Goldstein, "Police Discretion not to Invoke the Criminal Process: Low-Visibility Decisions in the Administration of Justice," *Yale Law Journal,* LXIX (March, 1960), 543–594; Herman Goldstein, "Police Discretion: The Ideal Versus the Real," *Public Administration Review,* XXIII (September, 1963), 140–148; John A. Gardiner, *Traffic and the Police: Variations in Law-Enforcement Policy* (Cambridge: Harvard University Press, 1969), chap. 6; James Q. Wilson, *Varieties of Police Behavior: The Management of Law and Order in Eight Communities* (Cambridge: Harvard University Press, 1968), chap. 8.

  [4] Wallace S. Sayre and Herbert Kaufman, *Governing New York City: Politics in the Metropolis* (New York: Russell Sage Foundation, 1960), chap. 19. See also Theodore J. Lowi, *At the Pleasure of the Mayor* (New York: Free Press, 1964).

  [5] Cf. the discussion of "attentive publics" in V. O. Key, Jr., *Public Opinion and American Democracy* (New York: Knopf, 1961), chap. 21; and Philip E. Converse, "The Nature of Belief Systems in Mass Publics," in David E. Apter, *Ideology and Discontent* (New York: Free Press, 1964), pp. 246–247: "Certain rather concrete issues may capture their [members of the mass public's] respective individual attentions and lead to some politically relevant opinion formation. This engagement of attention remains narrow however: Other issue concerns that any sophisticated observer would see as 'ideologically' related to the initial concern tend not to be thus associated in any breadth and number. The common citizen fails to develop more global points of view about politics."

  [6] Cf. the discussion of "latency" in public opinion in Key, *Public Opinion and American Democracy,* chap. 11; the concept of an "active sense of outrage" in Rogow and Lasswell, *op. cit.,* pp. 72–75; and James S. Coleman, *Community Conflict* (New York: Free Press, 1957), pp. 4–6.

  [7] Cf. the debate over the relative importance of constituents' attitudes and officials' perceptions of those attitudes in Warren E. Miller and Donald E. Stokes, "Constituency Influence in Congress," *American Political Science Review,* LVII (March, 1963), 45–56; Charles F. Cnudde and Donald J. McCrone, "The Linkage between Constituency Attitudes and Congressional

These questions concerning the direction and relevance of public attitudes toward law enforcement suggest several possible interpretations of the forty years of corruption which Wincanton has known. One possibility might be that Wincantonites wanted the wide-open gambling and prostitution which the Stern and Braun syndicates provided. Another might be that no one knew much about them (except for those who were going out of their way to find them). The following chapters attempt to test these views in several different ways. In this chapter, public attitudes will be examined in a relatively abstract or neutral context, relying on a survey conducted during a period in which the city government was making an honest and fairly successful attempt to keep organized crime out of the city. Chapter Five will explore law enforcement and corruption when they become matters of public controversy, i.e., when official corruption has been exposed and voters are asked to choose between candidates on the basis of law-enforcement and corruption issues. Chapter Five will also consider the agencies (state and federal prosecutors, "good government" groups, reform factions within the local parties, and the mass media) which sought to activate public hostility to corruption and inject it into local election campaigns. Chapter Six will consider the relationship between law-enforcement policies and the public by asking what difference it makes to a community whether its officials are corrupt or honest, or whether the police follow strict or lax enforcement policies.

In the following discussion of public attitudes toward gambling and corruption, four hypotheses will be examined:

1. Most residents know little about the specific policies followed by law-enforcement agencies or about the presence or absence of gambling and corruption. Information about law-enforcement policies and official activities, like information about other aspects of politics and public policy, will be highest among high-status residents, those who are most likely to read the newspapers and participate in politics.

2. Residents of the city are sharply divided in their attitudes toward gambling. Some view gambling as harmless recreation, while others see it as immoral or illegal. Most residents, however, support law-enforcement agencies and activities. Gambling is most tolerated or desired by women, long-term residents, and members of orthodox religious groups.

3. Mass attitudes toward corruption are unrelated to attitudes toward gambling. Hostility toward corruption is felt most strongly by upper-status

Voting Behavior: A Causal Model," *American Political Science Review*, LX (March, 1966), 66–72; Hugh Donald Forbes and Edward R. Tufte, "A Note of Caution in Causal Modeling," *American Political Science Review*, LXII (December, 1968), 1258–1264.

residents, possibly as a result of longer exposure to public norms through longer schooling.

4. Anticipating to a certain extent the discussion in Chapter Six of the consequences of long-term corruption, it is hypothesized that attitudes toward gambling and corruption will be affected by the length of residence in Wincanton. Long-term residents are more tolerant of gambling but less tolerant of corruption, since they have been exposed to more instances of official wrongdoing.

One *caveat* must be noted before presenting survey data related to these hypotheses. For a variety of reasons, answers given to interviewers may not be accurate reflections of the respondent's attitudes, particularly when topics such as gambling and corruption are involved. In a series of questions requiring identification of Wincanton officials and racketeers, interviewers felt that perhaps 10 percent of the respondents falsely professed ignorance in order "to keep out of trouble." In some cases, an answer will be given even though the respondent knows nothing or doesn't care about the question, simply because he wishes to avoid looking stupid or else wants to speed the interviewer on her way. In other cases, the response may be deliberately misleading in order to present what is assumed to be "the right answer," one which conforms to social norms or the presumed biases of the interviewer. Some responses may be misleading in other ways: hypothetical questions designed to test attitudes toward corruption may instead be testing the ability to recognize a norm violation in the stated facts, while questions aimed at identifying the overall frequency of gambling in the city may in fact test whether the respondent or his friends gamble. While these limitations and ambiguities are unavoidable, they will be noted as each set of data is presented and interpreted.

PUBLIC PERCEPTIONS OF LAW-ENFORCEMENT POLICY

What does the average citizen know about crime and law enforcement in his city? Nationwide surveys conducted for the National Crime Commission in 1966 indicate that crime is the second most important domestic problem in terms of attention paid by citizens (ranking only behind race relations); when asked *which* crimes they fear, respondents almost always cite crimes threatening personal safety.[8] Given this preoccupation with crimes of violence (or possibly theft), it would perhaps not be surprising if Wincantonites

---

[8] Jennie McIntyre, "Public Attitudes toward Crime and Law Enforcement," *Annals of the American Academy of Political and Social Science,* CCCLXXIV (November, 1967), 34–46.

knew little about the specific policies of their police department regarding gambling or prostitution. Publicly available information about the incidence of gambling and corruption, after all, has varied from year to year, and most details of the protection system underlying the Stern syndicate's activities have only come to light after a series of state and federal trials of city officials.

How much could the average resident of Wincanton have known about vice, gambling, and city hall corruption while they were taking place? Some idea can be gathered from the newspaper coverage during periods of corruption, and from the geographical distribution of each form of illegality. The dice game, for example, was in only one location (hidden and shifted periodically to escape federal attention) and relied primarily on out-of-town gamblers. Prostitutes were generally found only in two four-block areas in the city—semislum areas which no outsider was likely to visit unless he was specifically looking for the girls. The newspapers, however, gave extensive coverage to prostitution arrests and reports by the American Social Hygiene Association which detailed the extent of prostitution and venereal disease in the city; one series of illustrated articles forced the police to close (for a short period of time) several of the larger brothels. With regard to prostitution, therefore, it is likely that a majority of the adult population knew of the existence of commercialized vice; apart from innuendos in the papers, however, little information was available concerning payoffs to the police. It was not until 1964, *after* the election of a reform administration, that Stern and Walasek were indicted for extorting payments from a madam.

In comparison with the dice game and prostitution, public awareness of the existence of pinball machines, horse betting, and numbers writing must have been far more widespread. These mass-consumption forms of gambling *depended upon* accessibility to large numbers of persons, and bets could be placed in most corner grocery stores, candy shops, and cigar counters; payoff pinball machines were placed in most clubs and firehalls, as well as in bars and restaurants. Apart from one incident in which the president of the Volunteer Firemen's Association revealed that he had been asked to share in the costs of protection, however, there was nothing to suggest specifically to the average citizen that Irv Stern was paying to protect gambling until Police Chief Phillips began to testify in 1964—again, *after* the election of a reform mayor.

Public awareness of wrongdoing was probably *least* widespread as regards "free-lance" corruption—kickbacks on contracts, extortion, etc. Direct involvement was generally limited to officials and businessmen, and probably few of them knew anything other than that they themselves had been asked to pay off. Either from shame or fear of being prosecuted on bribery charges, or out of unwillingness to jeopardize a profitable contract, those who did pay off didn't want to talk. Except for an unsuccessful citizen's suit in 1965 seeking to void a purchase of fire trucks (the purchase on which Mayor Donnelly received a $2,000 "political contribution") and a newspaper article in 1961 implying that Donnelly and his council had received $500 on the sale of a city crane, no specific evidence of corruption was available to the public until Phillips was indicted in 1963 in connection with the car-towing contracts. In general, then, it can be said that even at a minimal level of knowledge—a general perception of some form of wrongdoing—mass awareness was quite limited. Specific knowledge—*this* official received *this* much to approve *that* contract—was only available after federal hearings in 1951 and the indictment of Phillips in 1963.

The 1966 Attitude Survey. If, therefore, it is unlikely that many residents of Wincanton had specific knowledge about local corruption while it was taking place, how much do they know *now*—after several years of reform and a series of trials, well covered in the newspapers, which revealed the nature of Stern-Donnelly-Walasek operations? In order to test the information and attitudes of Wincanton residents about gambling, law enforcement and corruption, a random sample of the Wincanton population was interviewed in 1966. One hundred and eighty usable interviews were obtained; the questions asked, and precise details of the sampling procedure, response rate, and characteristics of the respondents are contained in Appendix A.[9] In evaluating the results of this survey, it must be remembered that some residents will have forgotten things which they used to know and that some will be responding on the basis of information received from subsequent newspaper

---

[9] In light of our assumption that awareness and attitudes will vary according to the information available to respondents, we should specify at this point the conditions under which the survey took place. Interviewers came to Wincanton in August of 1966, two years and seven months after a reform mayor took control of the city hall. During the first two years of the Whitton administration, a series of well-publicized trials documented various aspects of Stern's involvement in city politics: extortion in the purchase of parking meters, firetrucks, and cars; the protection money demanded from prostitutes; and tax evasion related to Stern's gambling network. During 1964, 1965, and the first seven months of 1966, city and state police conducted well-publicized prostitution, lottery, and numbers raids, the last occurring three weeks before interviews began. Halfway through the interview period, a three-hour nationwide television program discussed the problem of organized crime in America. In a six-minute segment dealing with Wincanton, Dave Phillips, Mayor Walasek's police chief, detailed how he had paid Irv Stern $5,000 in order to become chief, how the protection system worked, and how he and his vice squad had staged phony gambling raids in order to placate newspaper demands for reform.

Anticipating the possibility that this television program would affect the survey results, separate samples of the Wincanton population were drawn for interviewing before and after the program (see Appendix A). Comparison of the responses of those who were interviewed before the program, those who saw it, and those who were interviewed afterwards but did not see it, show differences significant at the .05 level in two questions related to Police Chief

or courtroom exposés; the level of knowledge displayed now is probably greater than that which would have appeared in a survey in, say, 1962. However, it must also be remembered that individual questions may not test awareness of gambling or corruption in the form in which a respondent knew it; a man might not be able to recognize Irv Stern's name, for example, even though he bet every day with a numbers writer who worked for Stern.

A series of questions in the survey attempted to ascertain mass awareness of gambling and corruption by testing respondents' ability to identify leading politicians and racketeers, their perception of differences between the current (reform) and previous administrations, and their recollection of details of law-enforcement policies. First, to what extent were the respondents able to recognize leading public officials, racketeers, and law-enforcement agents? Table 4.1 lists, in descending order, the percentage of correct identifications. After the three most recent mayors, there is no clear differentiation in the ability of the respondents to identify public officials and syndicate racketeers; two-thirds knew Irv Stern and the local Congressman (who had held office for eighteen years). Only 40 percent knew either the current district attorney or the "bagman" or collector for the Stern syndicate. Among elected officials, the mayors were clearly better known than councilmen or district attorneys.

Which respondents were most familiar with these names? To simplify analysis of each respondent's level of information, an Information Index was constructed, giving two points for each correct identification and one point for each "close" identification. (Details of index construction and the distribution of scores are given in Appendix B.) Analysis of scores on the

Phillips (items 2 and 3). More importantly, however, difference-of-means tests reveal no significant differences (even at the .10 level) in five indices used in this chapter (items 4 through 8, below).

Survey Question or Mean Index Score	First Sample	Second Sample		Total Sample
		Saw Program	Didn't See	
1. Percentage correctly able to identify Police Chief Phillips	62%	78%	56%	63%
2. Percentage feeling that it was "right" for Phillips to testify against Stern and Walasek	55%	76%	58%	59%
3. Percentage feeling that it was right for Phillips to receive immunity from prosecution	21%	5%	15%	15%
4. Mean score on Information Index	19.90	22.24	17.47	19.45
5. Mean score on Perception of Gambling Index	5.01	4.94	4.49	4.79
6. Mean score on Perception of Bribability Index	10.95	11.62	11.41	11.18
7. Mean score on Tolerance of Gambling Index	3.96	4.16	3.67	3.88
8. Mean score on Tolerance of Corruption Index	7.39	7.13	6.91	7.13
Number of respondents	82	37	61	180

TABLE 4.1 *Identification of Wincanton Personalities*

Name	Percentage of Correct Identifications
Current Mayor Whitton	90
Former Mayor Walasek	86
Former Mayor Donnelly	73
Irv Stern	70
Prominent criminal lawyer	63
Congressman (held office eighteen years)	63
Ex-Police Chief Phillips	63
Stern lieutenant running numbers bank	63
Madam	62
Former district attorney	60
Former councilman and Democratic Party Chairman	54
Madam	48
Stern lieutenant, collector and enforcer	40
Current district attorney	40
Stern lieutenant running horse betting	31
Federal attorney who prosecuted Stern and Walasek	18

N = 180

Information Index showed no significant variations by age or sex; men were as likely as women, and the young as likely as the elderly, to have high or low information scores. Significant differences appeared, however, when the responses were analyzed in terms of social status (as measured by education) [10] and percentage of life spent in Wincanton. Both factors worked to increase the level of information; newcomers with little education knew

---

[10] The various indices used in this chapter were correlated with education, income, and a combined status scale based upon income, education, and occupation. As indicated below, income was generally the least powerful predictor of attitudes, possibly because forty-one of the seventy-nine respondents with incomes below $5,000 were retired. Education was a more powerful predictor of gambling attitudes, while the combined status measure was more powerful on corruption attitudes.

	Education			Income			Combined Status		
	Chi-square			Chi-square			Chi-square		
Index	X^2	Sig.	Tau	X^2	Sig.	Tau	X^2	Sig.	Tau
Tolerance of gambling	20.1	.01	.04	12.0	.30	.07	5.6	.10	.12
Perceptions of gambling	17.5	.01	—	7.7	.70	—	14.4	.01	—
Tolerance of corruption	17.6	.01	-.21	16.6	.10	-.22	21.4	.001	-.36
Perceptions of bribability	16.2	.02	.20	26.6	.01	.28	15.6	.001	.30

When the combined status measure was substituted for education in five tables (4.4, 4.6, 4.7, 4.13, and 4.14) used in this chapter, however, less significant chi-squares and taus emerged (for both gambling and corruption indices), so only the education results are presented in the text.

few of the names, while well-educated respondents who had spent most of their lives in the city knew most of the sixteen names.

A second dimension of public awareness of gambling and corruption is brought out by questions related to differences between the present (reform) administration and previous (corrupt) administrations. As in the questions testing identification of individuals, Table 4.2 shows a high level of ignorance concerning the district attorney's office; there is also a clearer ability (or willingness) to compare officials than to compare the availability of gambling. In questions 1, 3, and 5, however, clear perceptions emerge of differences in city administrations, police, and the role of "underworld elements and racketeers." Perceptions of differences between administrations are related to both social status and political party identification. Sixty-four percent of the high school graduates in the sample thought that the police force was better now, as compared with 55 percent of the less well educated. Seventy-three percent of the Republican respondents thought that the present (Republican-controlled) police force was better, as compared with 53 percent of the Democratic respondents.

While Table 4.2 showed a general perception that things had changed, the survey respondents had little specific knowledge about law-enforcement agencies and personnel; few recognized the names of district attorneys, and fewer had opinions about the district attorney's office than about the city administration or police department.[11] Other questions also revealed a low level of knowledge about recent controversial law-enforcement decisions. When asked, "As you remember it, who was it who decided that bingo should not be played in Wincanton?" 6 percent attributed the ban to the legislature, 45 percent correctly stated that a joint decision of Mayor Whitton and District Attorney Hendrichs (declaring that the state gambling law covered bingo) had led to the current crackdown, but 36 percent didn't know. Second, respondents were asked, "Which of the federal investigative agencies would you say was primarily responsible for most of the prosecutions of Wincanton people in the past ten years?" Thirty-one percent correctly cited the Internal Revenue Service, 20 percent mentioned the Federal Bureau of Investigation (which had only been involved in raiding the dice game), and 46 percent didn't know.

Perceptions of Gambling and Corruption. If the survey respondents felt that there had been a change in the character of the city government, what

---

[11] The likelihood that individuals will have general perceptions of governmental policies but little knowledge of their details is noted in Angus Campbell *et al., The American Voter,* abridged ed. (New York: Wiley, 1964), pp. 99–102.

TABLE 4.2 Perceptions of Differences Between City Administrations*

Question	Response				Total
	"Different"		"Same"	"Don't Know"	
1. "Some people say that the present city administration under Mayor Whitton is about the same as when Mayor Walasek was in office. Others disagree. What do you think? Is it about the same or different?	76% (136)		10% (18)	14% (25)	100% (179)
2. "How about the district attorney's office. Do you think that District Attorney Hendrichs' office is about the same as when Mr. French was district attorney, or is it different?"	36 (64)		13 (24)	51 (92)	100 (180)
	"Better"	"Worse"			
3. "Do you think the Wincanton police force now is better, about the same, or worse than it was under Mayor Walasek?"	59% (106)	7% (13)	22 (40)	12 (21)	100 (180)
	"Easier Now"	"Harder Now"			
4. "As compared with five years ago, do you think it's easier now, about the same, or harder					
—to place a bet on a horse race in Wincanton?"	2% (3)	52% (94)	12 (21)	34 (62)	100 (180)
—to find a dice game in Wincanton?"	1 (1)	57 (102)	8 (15)	34 (62)	100 (180)
	"Agree"		Disagree	Uncertain or "Don't Know"	
5. "Underworld elements and racketeers had (have) very little say in what the Wincanton city government					
—did when Mr. Walasek was mayor."	6% (11)		69% (125)	24% (44)	99 (180)
—does today."	54 (98)		13 (23)	33 (59)	100 (180)

*Number of respondents indicated in parentheses.

TABLE 4.3 *Perception of Popular Desires to Gamble*

"How Many People in Wincanton Like to——"	"Most"		"A Lot"		"Some"		"Almost None"		"Don't Know"		Total	
	%	N	%	N	%	N	%	N	%	N	%	N
"Play bingo?"	35	63	53	95	9	16	1	2	2	4	100	180
"Play the numbers?"	20	36	32	57	26	47	2	4	20	36	100	180
"Bet on horse races?"	10	17	39	70	28	51	2	4	21	38	100	180

were their estimates of gambling and corruption at the time of the interviews? (It must be kept in mind that the following questions were as likely to tap the personal experiences and attitudes of the respondents as some overall knowledge about the city.) When asked to judge the popularity of various forms of gambling, the respondents indicated that bingo was most popular; one-half also felt that "most" or "a lot" of local residents liked to play the numbers or bet on horses. A large proportion (20 percent) didn't know (or said they didn't know) the popularity of numbers and horse betting. Using the answers to these three questions in Table 4.3, an Index of Perception of Gambling was developed for the 126 respondents who gave answers other than "Don't know" for all three questions (see Appendix B). Analysis of scores on this index showed no variations by sex (men were as likely as women to see much or little gambling), but there were significant variations among social-status, age, and residence groups. Table 4.4 shows that perceptions of the popularity of gambling *decrease* as education increases; well-educated respondents were much less likely than the poorly educated to see gambling as being particularly popular in the city. Those who have spent most of their lives in the city are also more likely than the newcomers to find gambling popular. Further analysis shows that, regardless of education or residence status, elderly residents are more likely to believe that gambling is popular. Thus, 79 percent of the respondents over sixty, as compared with 55 percent of the younger respondents, thought gambling was very popular in Wincanton. While there is no way of knowing who *actually* gambles in Wincanton, these reported perceptions suggest that gambling (or at least these forms of gambling—bingo, the numbers, and horse betting) is most popular among low-income, low-education, and elderly residents. The lower perceptions of the long-term residents probably involve some comparative dimension; newcomers seem to see (whether correctly or not is impossible to say) more gambling in Wincanton than they saw (or recollect) in their former residence.

Table 4.2 indicated that the survey respondents believed the present reform administration to be significantly better than its predecessors. Their

TABLE 4.4 *High Perception of Gambling, by Education and Percentage of Life in Wincanton**

	Education							
	0–8 Years		9–12 Years		More Than 12 Years		Total	
Percentage of Life in Wincanton	%	N	%	N	%	N	%	N
Less than 80%	65	17	85	26	38	8	71	51
80% or more	68	19	58	45	18	11	55	75
Total	67	36	68	71	26	19	61	126

*This table shows the percentage of persons in each category who saw gambling as being very popular in Wincanton (a score of 7 or higher on the Perception of Gambling Index). Thus, 65 percent of the seventeen newcomers with low education saw gambling as being very popular. N.B., persons who answered "Don't know" to any one of the component questions were excluded from the index and this table. Pooling chi-squares between perceptions of gambling and education in the two residence categories produced a chi-square of 14.6; with four degrees of freedom, it was significant at the .01 level.

The chi-square test is a measure of the strength of relationship between two variables. Since its magnitude is affected both by the number of cases analyzed (*N*) and by the number of rows and columns, interpretations of chi-squares are dangerous. The chi-square in this table is significant at the .01 level, indicating that this distribution of responses would occur by chance only once in one hundred times. Pooling chi-squares from several tests (e.g., in the two residence categories) produces a measure of the overall relationship between two variables (e.g., education and perceptions of gambling) while controlling for a third (residence).

trust in it was hardly unlimited, however; Table 4.5 reveals that most respondents felt that city councilmen or policemen[12] would still take a bribe, although city officials had at least a slightly better reputation for honesty than did local businessmen or union officials. Using responses to these four questions, an Index of Perception of Bribability was constructed (see Appendix B). Variations in index scores were unaffected by sex, but trust (perception of low bribability, or "agree" responses to the four questions) was negatively related to social status, age, and percentage of life spent in the city. As might be expected, Table 4.6 shows that those who had spent most of their lives in this corrupt city were less trusting and more likely to expect bribery. While other studies have shown that the young and well educated are usually more trusting than others,[13] Tables 4.6 and 4.7 show that they were *less* trusting with regard to bribability in Wincanton. Given

---

[12] In 1966, a nationwide sample of 5,300 was asked the following question by the National Opinion Research Corporation: "Some people say that most policemen are honest and others say that most policemen take bribes and payoffs. Do you think the police around your neighborhood are almost all honest, mostly honest with a few who are corrupt, or are they almost all corrupt?" Fifty-eight percent felt that almost all were honest, 30 percent felt that most were honest, and 3 percent felt that almost all were corrupt. (Nine percent didn't know.) Phillip H. Ennis, *Criminal Victimization in the United States: A Report of a National Survey,* President's Commission on Law Enforcement and Administration of Justice, Field Survey II (Washington: Government Printing Office, 1967), p. 53.

[13] See Robert E. Agger, Marshall N. Goldstein, and Stanley A. Pearl, "Political Cynicism: Measurement and Meaning," *Journal of Politics,* XXIII (August, 1961), 477–506. For a review of the literature on class differences on civil liberties issues, see Key, *Public Opinion . . . ,* pp. 135–138.

TABLE 4.5 *Perceptions of Frequency of Bribery*

"No —— in Wincanton Would Take a Bribe"	Response									
	"Agree"		"Un-decided"		"Disagree"		"Don't Know"		Total	
	%	N	%	N	%	N	%	N	%	N
City councilman	11	19	34	61	48	86	7	12	100	178
Policeman	11	19	27	48	58	104	5	9	101	180
Businessman	9	16	25	45	61	110	5	9	100	180
Local labor union official	7	12	22	40	65	117	6	11	100	180

TABLE 4.6 *Low Perceptions of Bribability, by Education and Percentage of Life in Wincanton**

Percentage of Life in Wincanton	Education							
	0–8 Years		9–12 Years		More than 12 Years		Total	
	%	N	%	N	%	N	%	N
Less than 80%	55	31	38	40	25	12	42	83
80% or more	50	24	14	58	31	13	25	95
Total	53	55	23	98	28	25	33	178

*This table shows the percentage of persons in each category who perceived *little* bribability (a score of 1 through 9 on the Perception of Bribability Index); a high score, therefore, shows a high trust in the honesty of these people. Fifty-five percent of the thirty-one poorly educated newcomers, for example, saw little bribability and were highly trusting. Pooling chi-squares between perceptions of bribability and education in the two residence categories produced a chi-square of 22.2; with four degrees of freedom, it was significant at the .001 level. The Kendall's tau correlations between perceptions of bribability and education in the two residence categories were .22 and .19.

Kendall's tau, like the chi-square test, is a measure of the strength of relationship between two variables. It varies from .00 to ±1.00, with .00 indicating no relationship and 1.00 or −1.00 indicating a perfect positive or negative relationship.

TABLE 4.7 *Low Perceptions of Bribability, by Age and Education**

Education	Age							
	21–35		36–59		60 and Over		Total	
	%	N	%	N	%	N	%	N
0–8 years	38	8	56	16	53	32	52	56
9–12 years	19	37	24	41	30	20	23	98
More than 12 years	11	9	18	11	80	5	28	25
Total	20	54	31	68	47	57	33	179

*This table shows the percentage of persons in each category who perceived *little* bribability (a score of 1 through 9 on the Perception of Bribability Index); a high score, therefore, shows high trust. Thirty-eight percent of the eight young, poorly educated respondents, for example, saw little bribability and were highly trusting. Pooling chi-squares between perceptions of bribability and age in the three education categories produced a chi-square of 29.2; with 12 degrees of freedom, it was significant at the .01 level. The Kendall's tau correlations between perceptions of bribability and age in the three education categories were −.12, −.23, and −.45.

the city's history of corruption, it is not unlikely that the young and well educated feel most sharply the contrast between official norms and the recent conduct of Wincanton politicians and policemen.[14]

This information about public perceptions of law-enforcement policy supports the hypothesis that the average citizen recognizes gross variations, e.g., that the current administration is "different" from its predecessors, that it is harder to bet now, and that racketeers have less influence than they used to. More specific questions about law-enforcement agencies and policies, however, show a lessened ability to identify individuals or perceive change; few knew details concerning bingo policies or the activities of local or federal enforcement agencies. As expected, higher-status residents of the city are better informed (able to identify officials and racketeers) and are more

---

[14] One final question arises concerning this data. Do perceptions of bribability, as revealed through the four survey questions, actually reflect how frequently the four specified persons would take bribes, or do they reveal something about the attitudes of the respondents as well? Put another way, are variations among respondents indicators of how much they knew about Wincanton corruption, or do they reflect the respondents' psychological predispositions toward their city and the nature of man? The following table suggests that both factors are involved. While differences among education groups remain, trust clearly decreases as cynical attitudes toward politics increase. Since cynicism does not destroy the influence of education in predicting perceptions of bribability, cynicism and perceptions of bribability appear to be separate phenomena.

Low Perceptions of Bribability, by Cynicism and Education*

Cynicism Index Scores**	Years of Education							
	0–8		9–12		More than 12		Total	
	%	N	%	N	%	N	%	N
1 (Low)	60	10	36	14	40	10	44	34
2	67	15	41	27	43	7	49	49
3	53	17	15	34	0	7	24	58
4 (High)	29	14	9	23	*	2	18	39
Total	52%	56	23%	98	31%	26	33%	180

*This table shows the percentage of persons in each category with *low* perceptions of bribability (scores of 1 through 9 on the Perception of Bribability Index); a high percentage thus shows high trust in the honesty of the specified persons. Sixty percent of the ten respondents with little education and low cynicism scores, for example, had low perceptions of bribality. When less than five cases appeared in a cell, an asterisk (*) was substituted for the percentage figure. Pooling chi-squares between perceptions of bribability and cynicism in the three education categories produced a chi-square of 26.10; with eighteen degrees of freedom, it was significant at the .10 level. The Kendall's tau correlations between perceptions of bribability and cynicism in the three education categories were .23, .24, and .30.

**This Index of Cynicism was based on responses to three questions; one point was given for each "Agree" response to the following statements: "Most politicians in Wincanton take their orders from a few big men behind the scenes whom the public never really knows"; "Politicians spend most of their time getting reelected or reappointed." They were also given one point for each "Disagree" response to the following statement: "After politicians are elected to office in Wincanton, they usually keep their promises." One point was then added to each respondent's score to eliminate the zero category, and the final distribution of scores was:

1 (Low cynicism)		34	(19%)
2		49	(27%)
3		59	(33%)
4 (High cynicism)		38	(21%)
Total		180	(100%)

Inasmuch as Wincanton politicians have in the past been unusually untrustworthy, use of these questions as a measure of cynicism (as opposed to reality) is even more dangerous in Wincanton than in other cities. While reality and predispositions are inextricably mingled in the responses, these questions appear to test different matters than the questions used in the Perception of Bribability Index.

likely to assume corruptibility. Information also increases with length of residence in the city; long-term residents recognize more names and are more likely to assume corruptibility. They are *less* likely, however, to be impressed by the extent of gambling. The relationship between information and social status probably derives from two factors: newspaper readership, and thus exposure to information about local affairs, is higher among well-educated residents;[15] and higher-status (wealthy and well-educated) residents are more likely to participate in politics and to be interested in local matters.[16] This combination of media exposure and political involvement produces a greater ability to identify local names, whether of city officials or of racketeers. Familiarity is further increased by long-term residence in the city; those who have spent most of their lives in Wincanton are better able to identify local figures than are newcomers.[17]

ATTITUDES TOWARD LAW-ENFORCEMENT POLICY

In considering earlier questions concerning the level of public awareness of law-enforcement policies, it was necessary to recognize that a respondent might be lying about his familiarity with racketeers or gambling, that his information might be derived from reading the newspapers rather than from personal experience, and so forth. Analysis of questions designed to test attitudes toward enforcement policies presents further problems. For one thing, respondents vary in the degree to which an issue is salient to them. A woman whose husband has just squandered his pay check playing cards will consider a question about gambling in a different light than the minister's wife who has only heard of gambling as something which sinful people do. Moreover, respondents will vary in their interpretation of questions. One person asked about gambling may perceive symbolic issues ("Should the state condone games of chance?"), while others may think only of specific personal experiences ("Last night I bet my buddy a dollar that he couldn't finish a bottle of gin," or "The kids next door haven't eaten since their father lost his pay check in a poker game at the Elks' Club").[18] Among individuals

---

[15] See Key, *Public Opinion . . .* , pp. 348–349.

[16] The Kendall's tau correlation between scores on the Information Index and an Index of Political Participation was .27—participating respondents were better informed than nonparticipants.

[17] On the influence of length of residence in a community on political participation, see Robert E. Lane, *Political Life: Why and How People Get Involved in Politics* (New York: Free Press, 1959), pp. 267–269.

[18] A more complex categorization of values and value-orientations supportive of this distinction between specific and symbolic responses can be found in Clyde Kluckhohn, "Values and Value-Orientations in the Theory of Action: An Exploration in Definition and Classification," in Talcott Parsons and Edward A. Shils, eds., *Toward a General Theory of Action* (Cambridge: Harvard University Press, 1951), pp. 388–433.

with generally similar values, the response to a particular question may depend upon whether symbolic or specific ideas come to mind; even those who, on an abstract basis, grant the state the right to regulate games of chance may also defend the right of friends to gather for a kitchen-table poker game.[19] Even when a symbol of "law enforcement" is perceived, it may conflict with symbols of "friendship" ("It's just a bunch of buddies having a night out"), "charity" or "religion" ("The church needs to raise money through bingo games"), or "the right of privacy" ("The cops shouldn't go busting into people's houses").

This tension between symbolic and specific attitudes toward law-enforcement policy pervades responses to questions in the Wincanton survey dealing with gambling and corruption. When questions were phrased solely in terms of gambling, the respondents were quite tolerant, but tolerance diminished or disappeared when issues of nonenforcement or corruption appeared. Table 4.8 shows the frequency of tolerant responses to a series of questions dealing with gambling and other prohibited activities. It is clear that gambling (questions 1 through 5) is tolerated far more than narcotics, pornography, or prostitution (questions 10 through 12).[20]

Despite the fairly high degree of tolerance shown in the first five questions in Table 4.8, questions 6 through 9 show that tolerance diminishes when symbols of law enforcement (the police or district attorney) are introduced. Although 81 percent had favored the legalization of bingo, for example, only 24 percent felt that it should be tolerated if the legislature did *not* legalize it. This support for enforcement activities has appeared in a number of other

---

[19] Edelman notes that individuals often treat various forms of governmental regulations as games, symbolically accepting the rules and results of the game while calculating, on a specific basis, the probable costs of breaking the rules. Thus, a motorist could accept the validity of traffic laws on an abstract basis, yet choose, on the basis of the urgency of his trip or the reputation for efficiency of the local police, whether or not to speed; Murray Edelman, *The Symbolic Uses of Politics* (Urbana: University of Illinois Press, 1964), pp. 44–45.

[20] While, given the small size of the Wincanton sample and its overrepresentation of women and the better-educated residents of the city (see Appendix A), it is somewhat dangerous to compare these results with those from other areas of the country, it appears that Wincanton respondents were much more tolerant of gambling than were the 580 respondents in a 1953 Minnesota survey who were asked their personal opinions of gambling. Thirty-five percent of the Minnesota respondents felt that all gambling was wrong, 25 percent felt that some but not all gambling was wrong, and 38 percent felt that it was "all right for those who are interested" (Minnesota Survey 113, obtained, like the other surveys cited in this chapter, from the Roper Public Opinion Research Center at Williams College). Furthermore, in Minnesota surveys in 1949 and 1956, 62 percent and 59 percent of the respondents felt that bingo should be allowed in the state (Minnesota Surveys 77 and 144), as compared with 81 percent in Wincanton. In each of three nationwide surveys conducted between 1938 and 1963 by the American Institute of Public Opinion, between 48 percent and 51 percent favored the use of public lotteries "to help pay the costs of government" (American Institute of Public Opinion, Surveys 119, 163, and 672), although similar surveys conducted in Minnesota in 1948 and 1963 found only 31 percent and 42 percent in favor of state lotteries (Minnesota Surveys 53 and 224); 59 percent of the Wincanton respondents, by contrast, endorsed the lottery proposal.

TABLE 4.8 *Tolerance of Gambling and Corruption*

Question	Tolerant Response	% Toler-ant	% Intol-erant	% "Don't Know" or "Un-decided"
1. "How do you feel . . . do you think bingo should be allowed here, or not?"	"Allowed"	81	10	9
2. "Churches and other charitable organizations should be allowed to hold bingo games."	"Agree"	64	31	4
3. "The State of New Hampshire recently set up a lottery, and the proceeds are used to support public schools. Do you think (this state) should have a state lottery, or not?"	"Yes"	59	21	20
4. "Some people feel (this state) should legalize gambling. Others disagree. Do you think this should be done, or not?"	"Yes"	55	30	15
5. "Gambling is all right so long as local people, not outsiders, run the game."	"Agree"	50	36	14
6. "The police should not break up a friendly poker game, even if there is betting."	"Agree"	47	37	16
7. "If nobody has been hurt, a policeman should give a speeder a warning instead of a ticket."	"Agree"	34	56	9
8. "If the legislature does *not* legalize bingo, do you think the mayor and district attorney should continue to enforce the law against bingo, or not?"	"No"	24	67	9
9. "The Wincanton police today are concentrating on gambling too much."	"Agree"	18	56	27
10. "England now has legalized the use of narcotics in that drug addicts can get prescriptions for narcotics from doctors. Do you think this idea should be adopted in the United States or not?"	"Yes"	18	66	16
11. "There is way too much obscene literature in Wincanton today."	"Disagree"	17	57	27
12. "Some people say that the state should legalize prostitution. Would you agree or disagree?"*	"Agree"	14	82	4

*Question 12, dealing with prostitution, was given in a pretest interview schedule administered to a *nonrandom* sample of twenty-eight Wincanton residents, four of whom favored legalization. The pretest sample was strongly biased toward middle- and upper-middle-class residents. This question was dropped from the final interview schedule for reasons of time and fear that its subject matter would disturb respondents.

surveys. In 1966, the National Opinion Research Corporation asked a nationwide sample of 5,300 the following question: "In some places, vice and gambling bring a considerable amount of money to the community, even though they might give it a bad name. Do you think the police in such places should generally not interfere with vice and gambling at all, should act only on complaints, or should make every effort to stop the vice and gambling?" Seventy-three percent of the respondents felt that the police should try to stop the vice and gambling, 21 percent felt that they should only act on complaints, and only 2 percent thought they should not interfere. (Four percent didn't know.)[21] Seventy percent of the 875 respondents in a 1947 Minnesota survey approved of "Governor Youngdahl's campaign to wipe out all gambling devices, such as slot machines, in the state."[22] When asked, "If most of the people of Minnesota wanted lotteries and raffles, do you think state officials should let them go on, even though they are not legal, or do you think the people should observe the law now and ask the legislature to change it at the next session?", 85 percent of the respondents in a 1947 survey favored enforcement, while only 10 percent favored the continued operation of the games; 5 percent were undecided.[23] Finally, 1,000 respondents in a 1959 Texas survey were asked to choose between two hypothetical gubernatorial candidates, one of whom while serving as attorney general had closed down gambling joints in Galveston while the other had ignored them. Seventy-three percent were inclined to favor the reformer, while 12 percent favored his opponent; 15 percent were undecided. (Significantly, however, 60 percent of the respondents felt that the gambling issue alone was not a significant basis for choosing a candidate, feeling that other issues might be more important to them.)[24]

If the Wincanton respondents were not always thinking about "law-enforcement" issues when answering questions about gambling, what values were involved? Those who favored legalization of gambling or lotteries generally cited the current loss of revenues to other states: "A lottery helped New Hampshire and I think it could help us. If people can't gamble here, they just go to another place." "If you legalized gambling, there wouldn't be as much going around the corner. You should see all the license plates [from this state] at out-of-state racetracks." Others noted the value of gambling to churches and charitable organizations: "Fire companies and churches made money [from bingo] for good causes." "We could use the money [from a

[21] Ennis, *op. cit.*, p. 61.
[22] Minnesota Survey 42.
[23] Minnesota Survey 47.
[24] Texas Poll 1258.

lottery] for our schools." Those who wanted bingo to be legalized noted its function as a social event for the elderly: "It's a place for them to go and enjoy themselves." "My mother loved to play bingo; she would have died if they took it away while she was living. It was the only enjoyment she ever had." Those who *opposed* legalization of gambling occasionally gave a moral reason ("It degrades the morals of the people," or "It promotes a 'something for nothing' attitude"), but the most frequent argument was that gambling endangered the family income: "Husbands would spend money instead of using it for their families." "A man could lose his whole pay check if there were no limits." "There would be a lot of children going hungry." While many advocated legalization as a means of taking gambling out of the control of the rackets, a few respondents felt that racketeers would control even legalized gambling activities.

When questions in the Wincanton survey turned from gambling or gambling mixed with law enforcement to questions dealing specifically with official corruption, the tolerance of the respondents dropped markedly. Table 4.9 shows that as the implication of official wrongdoing becomes clear (as when cash rather than "presents" are involved), tolerance almost disappears.

TABLE 4.9 *Tolerance of Official Corruption*

Question	Tolerant Response	% Toler-ant	% Intol-erant	% "Don't Know" or "Un-decided"
1. "It's all right for a city official to accept presents from companies as long as the taxpayers don't suffer."	"Agree"	35	48	17
2. "It's all right for the mayor of a city to make a profit when that city buys some land so long as only a fair price is charged."	"Agree"	27	62	11
3. "A city official who receives $10 in cash from a company that does business with the city should *not* be prosecuted."	"Agree"	13	73	14

It might be pointed out that question 2 in Table 4.9 is somewhat ambiguous; a number of persons who agreed with that statement specified that the mayor had to *own* the land; he could not make a profit if someone else was selling it to the city. The intensity of the respondents' hostility toward corruption was brought out most strongly when the respondents were asked about the thirty-day jail sentences imposed on Irv Stern and Bob Walasek for extorting $10,500 on city purchases of parking meters. Eighty-six percent felt that the sentences were too light. When asked why they felt as they did, 32 percent felt that Walasek had "betrayed a public trust"; 18 percent gave an answer such as, "If it had been a little guy like me instead of a guy with pull like Walasek, I'd still be in jail."

Tolerance of Gambling. On the basis of five survey questions dealing with public policy toward gambling (legalization of gambling and bingo, a state lottery, "friendly poker," and gambling run by "local people rather than outsiders"), a Tolerance of Gambling Index was constructed for the 180 respondents (see Appendix B). Surprisingly, there was no correlation between tolerance and social status; the well educated were as tolerant of gambling as the poorly educated. As might be expected, however, Table 4.10 shows that respondents who felt that gambling was locally popular (high Perception of Gambling scores) were also tolerant of it and favored

TABLE 4.10 *High Tolerance of Gambling, by Perceptions of Gambling and Sex**

	Perception of Gambling Scores							
	"Don't Know" (0)		Low (1–6)		High (7–10)		Total	
Sex	%	N	%	N	%	N	%	N
Male	13	15	22	18	44	36	32	69
Female	34	38	53	30	60	42	49	110
Total	28	53	42	48	53	78	42	179

*This table shows the percentage of persons in each category who had high scores (5 or 6) on the Tolerance of Gambling Index; e.g., 13 percent of the fifteen men with 0 Perception of Gambling Index scores were highly tolerant of gambling. N.B., respondents listed in the "0" column answered "Don't know" to one or more of the index questions. (See Appendix B). Pooling the chi-squares between tolerance of gambling and perceptions of gambling in the two sex categories produced a chi-square of 3.76; with four degrees of freedom, it was significant only at the .50 level.

its legalization.[25] Respondents who perceive gambling to be popular in the city may well gamble themselves or know many who do, and thus have little difficulty concluding that it should be legalized. The higher tolerance of the female respondents is somewhat surprising, running counter to traditional assumptions that women are more moralistic than men. It is possible that women, even in talking with female interviewers, wanted to *appear* to be tolerant, e.g., by not depriving men of their fun, whether they in fact were or not. Some of this result can perhaps be explained by the fact that women are the most frequent bingo players, but since the other index questions dealt

---

[25] Paralleling this tendency of the Wincanton respondents who favored gambling to perceive it as popular, S. M. Lipset found that University of California students who supported a policy of the university regents tended (incorrectly) to perceive faculty support for their position, while anti-regents students (incorrectly) perceived public support for their views. See "Opinion Formation in a Crisis Situation," *Public Opinion Quarterly,* XVII (Spring, 1963), 20–46.

TABLE 4.11 *High Tolerance of Gambling, by Perceptions of Gambling, Sex, and Percentage of Life in Wincanton**

		Perception of Gambling Index Scores										
Percentage of Life in Wincanton	**Sex**	**Don't Know (0)**		**Low (1–6)**		**High (7–10)**		**Total**				
		%	N	%	N	%	N	%	N	%	N
Less than 80%	Male	10	10	10	10	25	16	17	36		
	Female	22	23	80	5	50	20	40	48	30	84
80% and over	Male	20	5	38	8	60	20	49	33		
	Female	53	15	48	25	68	22	57	62	54	95
Total		28	53	42	48	53	78			42	179

*This table shows the percentage of persons in each category who were highly tolerant of gambling (scores of 5 or 6 on the Tolerance of Gambling Index); 10 percent of the ten male newcomers with low perceptions of gambling, for example, had high Tolerance of Gambling scores. Pooling the chi-squares between tolerance of gambling and perception of gambling (excluding the "Don't know" respondents) in two residence and two sex categories produced a chi-square of 9.99; with four degrees of freedom, it was significant at the .05 level.

with gambling in general and even with poker (presumably a man's game), it is possible that traditional assumptions about feminine moralism have been wrong, at least as regards gambling.[26] Table 4.11 further shows that tolerance of gambling increases with residence in the city; in all sex and perception categories, long-term residents of the city are more tolerant than newcomers. This is hardly surprising; those who have spent most of their lives in a city in which gambling is popular (or believed to be popular) are less likely to find it objectionable than are those who may have come from cities where it was less widespread.

Finally, is it true, as is popularly assumed, that some religious groups are more tolerant of gambling than others? While there was no correlation between tolerance and frequency of church attendance, Table 4.12 clearly shows that members of orthodox religious groups are more tolerant than others even after the answers are controlled for sex and social status. While it is hard to believe that tolerance is related to orthodoxy per se, it may be that Catholic respondents had greater contact with gambling through church-sponsored bingo and other fund-raising events involving gambling.

Tolerance of Corruption. Table 4.9 shows that as indications of official corruption became clearer (as when cash presents to officials were involved),

---

[26] In the National Opinion Research Corporation study, however, 76 percent of the female respondents wanted the police to stop gambling, as compared with 70 percent of the men. Ennis, *op. cit.,* p. 62.

TABLE 4.12 *High Tolerance of Gambling, by Religion, Sex, and Education*

Variable	Religious Preference				
	Congregational, Episcopalian, Evangelical and Reformed, Evangelical United Brethren, United Methodist, United Church of Christ	Baptist, Presbyterian	Lutheran, Dutch Reformed	Catholic	All Religious Groups
Index of Christian Orthodoxy*	1.41	2.56	3.08	3.21	—
Percentage with high tolerance of gambling:**					
Total sample	26% (39)	31% (13)	48% (61)	53% (45)	43% (179)
Men	8 (13)	0 (6)	44 (23)	47 (19)	32 (69)
Women	35 (26)	57 (7)	50 (38)	58 (26)	50 (111)
Less than 12 years education	24 (21)	27 (11)	56 (32)	46 (28)	43 (110)
12 years education or more	28 (18)	— (2)	38 (29)	69 (17)	42 (69)

* The Index of Christian Orthodoxy for various religious groups was developed from a survey of 2,655 Christians by Charles Y. Glock and Rodney Stark in *Christian Beliefs and Anti-Semitism* (New York: Harper & Row, 1966), p. 13. In their four-point index, one point was given for each answer supporting the orthodox Christian position on the existence of a personal God, the divinity of Jesus Christ, the authenticity of Biblical miracles, and the existence of a devil. Wincanton respondents were not asked these questions, but were treated as having the orthodoxy score of Glock and Stark respondents of their denomination (e.g., Wincanton Episcopalian respondents were considered as having the mean orthodoxy score of Glock and Stark's Episcopalians). In a preliminary tabulation using seven denominational groupings ranked on orthodoxy, there was a perfect correlation with tolerance of gambling—highly orthodox groups were highly tolerant—with the exception of one group (Congregational–Evangelical and Reformed–United Church of Christ) which was more tolerant than its orthodoxy score would have predicted. In this table, all denominations with low (1.00–1.99) and medium (2.00–2.99) orthodoxy scores are collapsed and given orthodoxy scores proportional to their representation in the Wincanton sample; i.e., the Glock and Stark mean for Methodists was multiplied by the number of Wincanton Methodist respondents, the Episcopalian mean by the number of Wincanton Episcopalians, and so forth, and the sum was divided by the total number in the subgroup (e.g., 39 in the low orthodoxy group).

** This table shows the percentage of respondents in each category who were highly tolerant of gambling (a score of 5 or 6 on the Tolerance of Gambling Index). Fifty-three percent of the 45 Catholic respondents, for example, were highly tolerant. Where less than five cases appeared in a cell, a dash (—) was substituted for the percentage figure.

TABLE 4.13 *Low Tolerance of Corruption, by Age and Education**

	Education						
	0–8 years		9–12 years		More than 12 years		Total	
Age	%	N	%	N	%	N	%	N
21–35	43	7	51	37	89	9	57	53
36–59	38	16	20	41	64	11	31	68
60 and over	9	32	25	20	40	5	18	57
Total	22	55	33	98	68	25	34	178

*This table shows the percentage of persons in each category who had a *low* tolerance of corruption (scores of 1–5 on the Tolerance of Corruption Index); thus a high score on this table indicates a low tolerance of corruption. Forty-three percent of the seven young, poorly educated respondents, for example, had low tolerance of corruption. Pooling the chi-squares between tolerance of corruption and age in three education categories produced a chi-square of 24.47; with 12 degrees of freedom, it was significant at the .02 level. The Kendall's tau correlations between tolerance of corruption and education in three age categories were –.24, –.10 and –.19. The Kendall's tau correlations between tolerance of corruption and age in three education categories were .24, .24, and .33.

the tolerance of the respondents diminished. Tolerance decreased at different rates, however; some respondents became indignant at *any* indication of improper official activities, while others only rebelled when an exchange of money was specified. On the basis of four questions involving possible corruption (cancelling parking and speeding tickets, accepting presents, making a profit on the purchase of land, and a gift of $10 in cash), an Index of Tolerance of Corruption was constructed for the 180 respondents (see Appendix B). As anticipated, Table 4.13 shows that tolerance decreases as social status (education) increases. In addition, tolerance increases with age; regardless of education levels, older residents are more tolerant than respondents from other age groups. Furthermore, Table 4.14 shows that respondents who had spent most of their lives in Wincanton were less tolerant than the newcomers. Support for the laws (low tolerance of corruption) thus appears to be related to high social status, youth and long residence in the city. It may be that longer formal education gives upper-status residents greater contact with and reinforcement for official norms of public morality, and that the impact of education decreases as one gets older and further removed from formal schooling.[27] Citizen demands for official honesty are increased by exposure to the gross malfeasance that Wincanton has known; hardly becoming fatalistic or resigned to corruption, long-term residents of

[27] For a general discussion of the influence of education on political activities and attitudes, see Key, *Public Opinion . . . ,* chap. 13. See also the discussion of class variations in "public-regardingness" in James Q. Wilson and Edward C. Banfield, "Public-Regardingness as a Value Premise in Voting Behavior," *American Political Science Review,* LVIII (December, 1964), 876–887.

TABLE 4.14 *Low Tolerance of Corruption, by Education and Percentage of Life in Wincanton**

| | Percentage of Life in Wincanton | | | | | |
| | Less than 80% | | 80% or More | | Total | |
Education	%	N	%	N	%	N
0–11 years	20	55	33	54	27	109
12 years or more	43	28	51	41	48	69
Total	28	83	41	95	35	178

*This table shows the percentage of persons in each category with low tolerance of corruption (scores of 1–5 on the Tolerance of Corruption Index); thus a high score on this table indicates a low tolerance of corruption. Twenty percent of the 55 poorly educated newcomers, for example, had a low tolerance of corruption. Pooling the chi-squares between tolerance of corruption and education in the two residence categories produced a chi-square of 7.9; with two degrees of freedom, it was significant at the .02 level. The Kendall's tau correlations between tolerance of corruption and education in the two residence categories were –.20 and –.18.

the city seem to have a heightened sensitivity to situations possibly involving misconduct.

Conclusions. Earlier, it was asked whether widespread local corruption should be attributed to the values and attitudes of city residents. The evidence suggests that the answer is both yes and no. As an abstract issue, most people in Wincanton see little wrong with gambling. They believe that many forms of petty gambling are locally popular and seldom criticize those who indulge in them. They question the wisdom of the state's antigambling laws and would support the legalization of most forms of gambling.

As anticipated, upper-status residents of Wincanton were better informed about politics and corruption (although their information probably came from reading the newspapers rather than from actual contact with gamblers or official corruption) and were less tolerant of official corruption. Also as expected, those who gambled and those who had spent most of their lives in the city were most tolerant of gambling. However, those who had spent most of their lives in Wincanton were less tolerant of corruption than were those who had lived elsewhere.

While the Wincantonites' rejection of current gambling laws provides support for the thesis that corruption facilitates the realization of popular values —that the Stern-bribed mayors and policemen were simply giving Wincantonites the gambling they wanted—the survey clearly shows that the residents of Wincanton did not tolerate corruption per se. Whenever symbols of law enforcement and official morality were brought into survey questions, most respondents opted for public norms of morality. While some of the survey respondents were slow to perceive that corruption might arise from relationships between officials and persons doing business with the city, they clearly chose honesty and law enforcement when they recognized the nature of the relationship.

If, then, the attitudes of the public toward law enforcement policy depend on the way in which issues are perceived—whether "gambling" or "corruption" is thought to be the issue in question—it must be asked under what conditions the general public will come to see a "corruption" issue in local politics. When will normally noninvolved citizens become interested in questions of law-enforcement policy? How will such interest be translated into a new set of official policies? Chapter Five considers these questions.

Corruption as a
Political Issue

*It took a lot of work, but we were finally able to apprehend
and convict Irv Stern, Klaus Braun, and the other big racketeers in Wincanton. But we were never able to solve the
political problem—City Hall officials were always against
us.* —A FEDERAL LAW-ENFORCEMENT AGENT

UNDER ordinary conditions, a police official has a great
deal of freedom in deciding what policies to follow. So long as large (and
vocal) interests within the community do not believe themselves to be ad-
versely affected by police practices, a "zone of indifference"[1] exists within
which the official can choose to stress certain laws, ignore others, and so
forth. Where demands for the enforcement of a particular law are weak, or
where proenforcement demands are matched by equal demands for nonenforcement, the official will be especially free to act as he chooses. His freedom of choice, of course, will also be influenced by the extent to which police policies are known to the public; unless citizens *know* that the police are
ignoring particular forms of illegal behavior, they will be likely to assume

---

[1] James Q. Wilson, *Varieties of Police Behavior: The Management of Law and Order in
Eight Communities* (Cambridge: Harvard University Press, 1968), p. 233, citing Chester A.
Barnard, *The Functions of the Executive* (Cambridge: Harvard University Press, 1938), pp.
168–169. On public indifference to and ignorance of police *traffic* policies, see John A. Gardiner,
Traffic and the Police: Variations in Law-Enforcement Policy (Cambridge: Harvard University
Press, 1969), chap. 6.

from the mere presence of the police and of the laws forbidding such behavior that their interests are being protected.[2]

The zone of public indifference to police activities is particularly wide in the case of enforcement of gambling and prostitution laws. As "crimes without victims,"[3] gambling and prostitution cause serious harm to few individuals; on the contrary, in most medium- and large-sized cities, a substantial number of persons will be seeking freedom to gamble or to find prostitutes. While tolerance of gambling is probably somewhat higher in Wincanton than in other cities, the survey results presented in Chapter Four suggest that almost as many people disagree with as support antigambling legislation. In addition, while there was a great deal of generalized support for law-enforcement agencies, there was relatively little knowledge about specific police practices. Interest in police activities seemed concentrated on protection against violence, and the subject of gambling only captured public attention when popular pastimes such as bingo for the elderly or gambling at church carnivals were threatened. Awareness of the corruption which had made gambling possible, and of the free-lance corruption which was also taking place, was even more restricted. Given the low salience to the average citizen of police gambling policies, and the confused and contradictory views as to what policies should be followed, therefore, it is not surprising that the Wincanton officials corrupted by the Stern syndicate were not greatly afraid of public reprisals. Control over city officials, police, judges, and prosecutors was usually a sufficient guarantee that the Stern organization could operate without interference.

While this pattern of corruption of city officials and of the setting of law-enforcement policy by a quite limited number of people has been a dominant characteristic of Wincanton politics over the last forty years, the general public has occasionally become involved in shaping enforcement policies. On three occasions, mayoral candidates campaigned on a platform of destroying organized crime, defeated heavily favored opponents identified with the syndicates, and then used the city police force to eliminate organized gambling and prostitution. In other years, charges of corruption led to the defeat of city officials, but the victorious candidates proved to be as corrupt as their predecessors. Since these election campaigns marked the only points at which latent mass hostility to corruption was brought into the local decision-making process (even if unsuccessfully in the latter set of elections), they raise a number of questions about corruption as a political issue rather

---

[2] Murray Edelman, *The Symbolic Uses of Politics* (Urbana: University of Illinois Press, 1964), chap. 2.

[3] Edwin M. Schur, *Crimes Without Victims* (Englewood Cliffs, N.J.: Prentice-Hall, 1965).

than as a matter of abstract public opinion. Under what conditions will corruption become an important issue in local elections? What agencies publicize the presence of corruption and provide vehicles (candidates) through which voters can act upon their anticorruption values? Why have periods of reform in Wincanton been of such short duration? Three hypotheses will be considered: (1) corruption becomes a significant issue in local politics as the result of startling "critical events" which shift the level of popular thought from a pragmatic to a symbolic plane; (2) following these critical events, reform political organizations can fairly easily use the issue of corruption to oust incumbent officials; but (3) honesty (hostility to gambling and corruption) is not by itself sufficient to sustain a political movement, so purely "reform" administrations will quickly lose power.

Local Elections in Wincanton. Two facts stand out in any analysis of electoral politics in Wincanton. The first is that it is a solidly Democratic city; there are about two registered Democrats for every Republican in the city, and about three Democrats for every two Republicans in Alsace County as a whole. As can be seen in Table 5.1, Democratic candidates have easily won all local elections since World War II with the exception of those held in 1951 and 1963. A second recurring phenomenon in Wincanton politics is the issue of official corruption. In every election since World War II, Re-

TABLE 5.1 *Voting Patterns in Wincanton Elections*

Year	Winning Mayoral Candidate	Party	Percentage of Votes* Cast for Democratic Candidates
1947	James Watts	Democratic	58
1949	(Council election)	Democratic	53
1951	Harold Craig	Republican	46
1953	(Council election)	Democratic	65
1955	Eugene Donnelly	Democratic	61
1957	(Council election)	Democratic	59
1959	Robert Walasek	Democratic	59
1961	(Council election)	Democratic	57
1963	Edward Whitton	Republican	43
1965	(Council election)	Democratic	63
1967	Ian Redford	Democratic	56

*This column shows the percentage of the two-party vote received by the Democratic candidate. In 1947, the last year in which the Socialist Party polled a substantial vote in city elections, the Democratic candidate received 37 percent of the three-party vote, the Socialist 36 percent, and the Republican 27 percent.

publican candidates have charged that their Democratic opponents participated in corrupt activities or were likely to tolerate the operations of the Stern syndicate.[4] A 1963 Republican campaign newsletter, for example, charged that the Walasek administration had protected the Stern syndicate ("Does the Cosa Nostra Reach into Alsace County?") and had received a large kickback from a sale of city property ("GOP Uncovers Gigantic Land Giveaway!"). In both 1951 and 1963, Republican candidates won office on the corruption issue, and proceeded to destroy organized gambling.

In many of the years that Republicans attacked Democratic alliances with the syndicates, a number of candidates in Democratic party primaries made similar charges against their opponents. During the 1959 primaries, for example, Bob Walasek announced that he had been "approached several times by the emissaries of the racket and vice bosses of Wincanton to withdraw from the mayoralty race," and declared that Stern was working for the re-election of Mayor Donnelly. (In his inaugural address the following January, Walasek pledged, "We will not tolerate organized gambling, vice, and racketeering, and under no circumstance will coercion be used by the police department to force payoffs.") In the 1963 primary election, incumbent Walasek finished third, behind two men who criticized his toleration of Stern. The 1967 primary saw the narrow defeat (by a margin of 132 votes out of 15,000) of a heavily favored candidate who had been a councilman during the Walasek administration; the victorious challenger based his primary campaign on an identification of his opponent with the corruption of the Walasek era.

In each of these five campaigns, the issue of corruption led to the defeat of an incumbent mayor or heavily favored "organization" candidate. The 1959 election of Walasek, of course, proved to be a Pyrrhic victory for reform voters, since he continued Mayor Donnelly's policy of cooperating with the Stern syndicate, and many Wincantonites felt that the Democratic nominee in 1963 would have proved to be just as corrupt. It must nevertheless be noted that Wincanton voters consistently rejected candidates charged with flagrant corruption.

Critical Events. To understand the forces producing the election of these "reform" candidates, let us look more closely at the events surrounding each election campaign.

---

[4] That corruption in Wincanton was predominantly carried out by Democrats should not lead the reader to assume that the Democratic Party has a monopoly on corruption. At the turn of the century, Lincoln Steffens found cities with as many corrupt Republicans as Democrats. Lincoln Steffens, *Autobiography* (New York: Harcourt, Brace, 1931). In Newburgh, New York, James Q. Wilson recently found successive Republican and Democratic politicians tolerating wide-open gambling and prostitution. See *Varieties of Police Behavior*, pp. 244–245.

—In June of 1951, a Congressional committee investigating organized crime held hearings on the activities of the Stern syndicate. The Wincanton police chief testified that although he had heard "rumors" of local gambling, it was the "policy of the department to act on complaints only," so he had never attempted to arrest Stern or Braun. The committee's report, issued nine weeks before the 1951 city elections, outlined the structure of the Stern syndicate and concluded that Wincanton was a "classic example of political strangulation of a police department at the behest of gambling interests seeking to thwart any interference with their activities."

—Twice during the Donnelly administration (1956–1960), federal agents raided bookmakers operating in a tavern owned by Donnelly. Internal Revenue Service agents closed a large illicit distillery, leading to grand jury questioning of Donnelly, his city solicitor, and a city councilman. In the year prior to the 1959 primary elections, members of the Stern syndicate were tried on extortion charges for threatening pinball-machine distributors if they failed to pay protection money.

—During the Walasek administration (1960–1964), federal agents raided Stern's numbers and horse-betting operations, sending Stern to prison for four years. A year-long investigation by attorneys from the Organized Crime and Racketeering Section of the Department of Justice led to the indictment, one week before the 1963 primary elections, of Walasek's police chief. During the general election campaign, Stern and Walasek were indicted on charges of extortion in two city purchases of parking meters, and twelve racketeers were convicted on gambling charges stemming from the 1962 F.B.I. raid on Stern's dice game.

—During the first two years of the Whitton administration (1964–1968), petty gamblers and prostitutes were arrested by the city police, and Walasek and Stern were convicted of extortion. Two days before the primaries in 1967, the National Crime Commission issued its *Task Force Report: Organized Crime,* with an eighteen-page study of crime and corruption during the Donnelly-Walasek period. Wincanton newspapers quoted extensively from the report, with headlines such as "U.S. Crime Study Pinpoints Wincanton and its Apathy," and "Crime Fighters Zero in on Us."

Why might these events have influenced voting in city elections? First, they gave the voters *specific* information about the corruption which permitted the Stern organization to survive. It was noted in Chapter Four that few Wincantonites could have known much about the protection system, apart from the vague assertions which repeatedly appeared in the local papers. ("There is no question but that the rackets pack here will be trying its best to grab control again of City Hall and the courthouse," warned one newspaper editor in a typical front-page column in 1966).[5] Although these critical events varied in their proximity to election day (two days before the 1967 primaries versus twelve to eighteen months before the primaries in 1959), and in their relationship to the candidates (events prior to the general election of 1951 and the primary elections of 1959 and 1963 pointed out men actually running for office, while the other events only condemned the Walasek administration in general), they all provided more specific information about corruption than had previously been available.[6]

The informative function of these critical events was probably increased by the fact that they emanated from authoritative, purportedly neutral agencies—a Senate committee, attorneys from the Department of Justice, and the National Crime Commission. Because of the source of these events, they may have been noticed by a higher proportion of the population ("If the federal government has to come in here to clean things up, it must be pretty serious"), and a higher proportion may have believed the charges ("It's not just as if the *Gazette* were 'crying wolf' again—it's *Washington* saying that Walasek is a crook").

A second consequence of these critical events, beyond the communication of information about corruption, was the stimulation of what Rogow and Lasswell term an "active sense of outrage." The publicizing of these events by the mass media served to remind residents of the public norms of official morality and activated their otherwise latent support for these norms.[7] After the activation of the norms and an itemizing of the officials' violations of them, critical events revealed specific betrayals of public expectations as to how officials should act and suggested vehicles (voting for other candidates) by which expected behavior might be reinstated. While it had been

---

[5] In his study of American politics eighty years ago, Lord Bryce observed, "The people see little and they believe less. True, the party newspapers accuse their opponents of such offenses, but the newspapers are always reviling somebody; and it is because the words are so strong that the tale has little meaning. . . . The habit of hearing charges promiscuously bandied to and fro, but seldom probed to the bottom, makes men heedless." See James Bryce, *The American Commonwealth*, Vol. II (London: Macmillan, 1889), 204.

[6] Robert E. Lane points out that citizens assume that politicians will always be *slightly* corrupt, and so they *notice* corruption only when its scale exceeds these "normal" expectations. "Their reactions to reports of governmental corruption is, generally speaking, a tolerant one, certainly not indignant, not moralistic, possibly insufficiently censorious. It is marked by a belief that *the system encourages corruption,* that it is somehow 'natural' to politics." See *Political Ideology: Why the American Common Man Believes What He Does* (New York: Free Press, 1962), p. 335 (emphasis in original).

[7] For a discussion of the role of the mass media in limiting the scope of a controversy and in isolating deviant positions, see James S. Coleman, *Community Conflict* (New York: Free Press, 1957), pp. 24–25.

possible, prior to these critical events, to consider gambling in pragmatic terms ("It's only a bunch of friends getting together to play poker"), critical events shifted the voter's frame of reference to the symbolic level ("Will our officials enforce the laws?").[8] With the issue having been restated in this form, most voters were *forced* to choose between, as Rogow and Lasswell put it, "the minority norm or the inclusive norm"; pragmatic toleration of both sets of values was no longer possible.[9] As indicated by the survey results summarized in Table 4.8, citizen support for law enforcement will tend to override desires to gamble or to participate in other illegal activities when the conflict between the two is clearly stated. When critical events reveal that citizens have been wrong in assuming that laws and law-enforcement agencies were protecting their interests, their normal quiescence and noninvolvement disappear and they become actively involved in the restoration of official morality.[10] Although it is impossible to prove which was the more decisive factor, it is likely that Wincanton voters rejected mayors Donnelly and Walasek not because they had tolerated gambling and the Stern syndicate but because they had taken bribes to do so; corruption was a greater violation of public norms than the nonenforcement of the state's gambling laws.

Voting Patterns Following Critical Events. In the Democratic primary elections of 1959, 1963, and 1967, incumbent mayors or favored "organization" candidates were defeated by avowed reformers; in the general elections of 1951 and 1963, Republican candidates won despite a two-to-one Democratic majority in voter registration. Critical events activated voter hostility to official corruption and caused sufficient changes in voting to lead to the election of reform officials. These voting changes raise several questions. First, did normally Democratic voters switch sides or simply decide not to vote, thus giving the Republicans a majority? Second, did voting changes occur predominantly within one segment of the Wincanton population or were they more widely distributed? In Chapter Four it was noted that support for public norms of official morality (low Tolerance of Corruption scores) were highest among upper-status residents and among those who

---

[8] The process by which factions in a conflict tend to escalate the terms of controversy by appealing to broad societal norms is discussed in E. E. Schattschneider, *The Semi-Sovereign People: A Realist's View of Democracy in America* (New York: Holt, Rinehart and Winston, 1960).

[9] Arnold A. Rogow and Harold D. Lasswell, *Power, Corruption, and Rectitude* (Englewood Cliffs, N.J.: Prentice-Hall, 1963), pp. 72–73. For a discussion of the reasons law enforcement is usually regarded as a game (in which rule-breaking is regarded as an acceptable strategy) rather than as an abstract issue, see Edelman, *op. cit.*, chap. 3.

[10] Edelman, *op. cit.*, p. 167.

had spent most of their lives in the city. Do similar variations appear in the voting patterns in elections following critical events?

Two factors limit the extent to which these questions can be answered through an analysis of election data. Since Wincanton primaries are usually wide-open battles among a variety of candidates each of whom is usually campaigning on the basis of his personality and his ability to deliver local services (street improvements, playgrounds, etc.), it is almost impossible to isolate "reform" and "antireform" patterns in primary voting data. Second, since there is little information available concerning the behavior of *individual* voters (only 51 percent of the 180 survey respondents recalled having voted in 1963), analysis must be confined to the actions of aggregates—groups of voters. While it can legitimately be noted that 48 percent of the voters of the twentieth ward supported a reform candidate, no one can be sure that the reform voters were the persons identified by the census as being laborers or of Italian descent. The most that can validly be concluded from a study of aggregate data is that groups (e.g., voters in a ward or precinct) with particular characteristics are more likely than other groups to support certain candidates.[11]

Keeping these dangers in mind, there is some support for the propositions that (1) the cross-pressures[12] of identification with the Democratic Party and hostility to corruption reduced the turnout of normally Democratic voters in 1951 and 1963; (2) a number of normally Democratic voters switched to support Republican candidates in these two years; and (3) hostility to corruption (and thus a tendency to switch to support Republican candidates) was felt most strongly by upper-status and long-time residents of the city. Limited evidence to support the first two propositions can be found in Tables 5.2 and 5.3. Table 5.2 shows that there was a *higher* voter turnout in 1951 and 1963 than in other years, both in absolute numbers and as a percentage of the registered voters.[13] While the total vote was higher in

[11] On the problems involved in analyzing aggregate data, see W. S. Robinson, "Ecological Correlations and the Behavior of Individuals," *American Sociological Review,* xv (June, 1950), 351–357; Austin Ranney, "The Utility and Limitations of Aggregate Data in the Study of Electoral Behavior," in *Essays on the Behavioral Study of Politics* (Urbana: University of Illinois Press, 1962), pp. 91–102; Heinz Eulau, "Segments of Political Science Most Susceptible to Behavioral Treatment," in James C. Charlesworth, ed., *Contemporary Political Analysis* (New York: Free Press, 1967), pp. 32–50.

[12] The literature on the impact of cross-pressures on political participation is discussed by Robert E. Lane, *Political Life: Why and How People Get Involved In Politics* (New York: Free Press, 1959), pp. 197–203. For an analysis of the relationship between voter turnout in local elections and structural and demographic characteristics of American cities, see Robert R. Alford and Eugene C. Lee, "Voting Turnout in American Cities," *American Political Science Review,* LXII (September, 1968), 796–813.

[13] Under the state law, registration for voting requires residence of one year in the state and sixty days in the election district. Registration closes six weeks before the general elections. Voters must declare party affiliation when they register, if they wish to vote in the primaries, but affiliation may be changed at any time between the November general elections and the spring primaries.

TABLE 5.2 *Voter Registration and Turnout in Wincanton Elections*

	Voter Registration			Voting			
Year	Total	Democrats	% Demo-cratic	Total	Votes for Democrats	% Demo-cratic	% Turnout
1947	47,826	30,765	64	31,402	11,588	58*	66
1951	48,415	31,688	65	35,790	14,018	46	74
1955	45,303	29,880	66	32,238	18,554	61	71
1959	44,674	30,899	69	31,394	18,501	59	70
1963	45,236	32,059	71	32,843	14,279	43	73
1967	40,286	28,704	71	28,666	15,973	56	71

*In 1947, the Democratic candidate for mayor won a plurality in a three-way contest with a Republican and a Socialist; he received 37 percent of the total vote, but 58 percent of the combined Republican and Democratic vote.

TABLE 5.3 *Relationship Between Voter Turnout and Support for Democratic Candidates*

Year	Correlation*
1951	$r = -.61$
1955	.04
1959	—.33
1963	—.46
1967	—.41

*This table shows the Pearsonian product-moment correlation between the percentage of registered voters who actually voted and the percentage of the total vote cast for the Democratic candidate in seventy-seven Wincanton precincts.

these years, Table 5.3 shows that the normally negative relationship between turnout and support for Democrats (turnout is almost always higher in precincts supporting Republicans) was even stronger in 1951 and 1963. The higher total turnout in these years and the variations shown in Table 5.3 probably are based upon both a higher turnout of Republicans, sensing possible victory, and a reduced turnout of Democrats, cross-pressured by the charges of corruption leveled against the Democratic nominees. Some evidence of vote-switching by Democrats can be seen in the ticket-splitting which occurred in 1963 (but not in 1951): while receiving enough votes to win, the two Republican candidates for the city council each received 1,700 fewer votes than the Republican candidate for mayor.

Who switched? Were the pressures of critical events felt more strongly by one group of voters, such as the wealthy or well educated, than by others? Since a vote for "public morality" in 1951 or 1963 was also a vote for the

FIGURE 1 *Relation Between Normal Democratic Vote and Vote for Democratic Candidate in 1951*

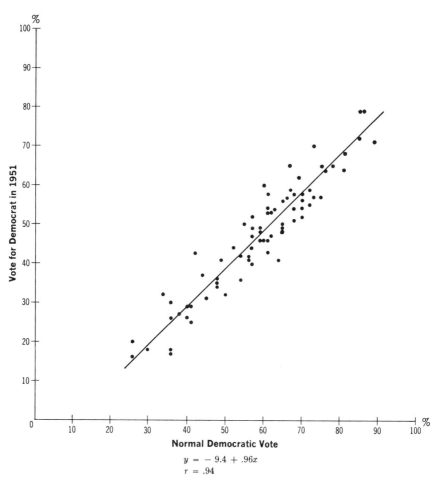

$$y = -9.4 + .96x$$
$$r = .94$$

Republican candidate, it is necessary to distinguish between voters who would support *any* Republican and voters who were specifically interested in restoring official morality; therefore, information must be drawn from precincts which shifted significantly from their normal voting patterns. Figures 1 and 2 suggest that voting in 1951 and 1963 was a direct function of *normal* party voting;[14] there was a fairly uniform (about 9 percent in 1951, about 6 percent in 1963) decline in Democratic voting in each precinct

---

[14] The "normal Democratic vote" for each precinct is defined as the mean percent voting for Democratic candidates in three elections *not* involving critical events—the general elections for mayor in 1955 and 1959 and for governor in 1962. Product-moment correlations (for seventy-seven precincts) among the three elections comprising the normal vote were .96, .95, and .97.

FIGURE 2 *Relation Between Normal Democratic Vote and Vote for Democratic Candidate in 1963*

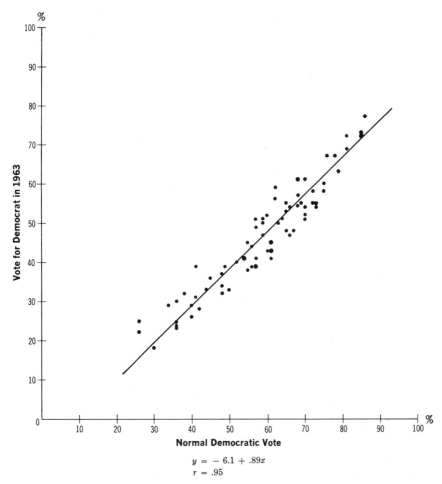

$$y = -6.1 + .89x$$
$$r = .95$$

rather than a sharp decline in some and no decline in others. The slopes of the regression equations (.89 and .96) indicate an almost perfect parallel between the normal vote and the vote following critical events; heavily Democratic precincts were neither more nor less likely to shift than heavily Republican precincts.

Although normal party voting explains most of the voting patterns of the 1951 and 1963 elections, some support for the conclusions of Chapter Four can be found when relationships between voting and measures of mobility and social status are controlled to isolate the effects of normal party voting. Based on characteristics of thirteen districts of Wincanton, Table 5.4 shows

TABLE 5.4 *Relationships Between Democratic Voting in 1951 and 1963 and Measures of Mobility and Social Status**

	Demographic Variables	
Election	**Percentage New to Alsace County Since 1955**	**Median Family Income**
1951 voting for Democratic candidate:		
Simple correlation	—.69	—.53
Partial correlation, controlling for normal Democratic vote	.17	—.30
1963 voting for Democratic candidate:		
Simple correlation	—.61	—.54
Partial correlation, controlling for normal Democratic vote	.54	—.29
Correlation with normal Democratic vote	—.72	—.49

*For the purposes of the analysis in Table 5.4, the City of Wincanton was divided into thirteen units with congruent census tract and voting district boundaries; eleven of the units had populations between 2,700 and 9,700, and two units had between 10,000 and 15,000 residents. After collapsing data from smaller units so as to identify the aggregate characteristics of each unit (normal Democratic vote, median income, etc.), correlation analysis showed a product-moment correlation of .98 between normal Democratic voting and voting for the Democratic candidate in 1951, and .97 between normal Democratic voting and voting for the Democratic candidate in 1963. I am indebted to Sandra Olson and Melvin T. Katz for performing the computations underlying this analysis.

the simple correlation between these demographic characteristics and the normal Democratic vote, the simple correlation between these demographic variables and voting in the two years, and the partial correlations when the simple demographic-voting correlations are controlled for the normal Democratic vote. In both years, support for Democratic candidates is positively related to population mobility—districts with high proportions of residents new to the county since 1955 were more likely to continue to support Democratic candidates. Recalling the earlier discussion of the effects of continued residence in a city with a corrupt history like Wincanton's, it appears that the critical events of 1951 and 1963 were felt less sharply by new residents than by long-term residents. Supporting the earlier finding that upper-status residents were less tolerant of corruption than lower-status residents, Table 5.4 also shows that districts with high median family incomes tended to reduce their support for Democratic candidates.[15] Thus, supporting the survey results presented in Chapter Four, these voting data suggest that while normal party voting patterns are the best predictors of voting following critical events, upper-status (high-income) districts are more likely than others to

---

[15] Similar results appeared when education was substituted for income in this analysis. When the correlation between 1963 voting and percentage with more than twelve years of education was controlled for both normal Democratic voting and percentage from a different county, a partial correlation of —.13 appeared.

respond to charges of corruption by turning to Republican reformers, as are districts with high proportions of long-time residents.

The Cycle of Corruption and Reform. The last twenty-five years of Wincanton politics, summarized in Table 5.1, show a cyclical pattern of growth and decline of reform. The high points of Democratic power were the elections of 1947, 1953, and 1965. The ensuing years saw a steady erosion of Democratic strength until the Republicans, capitalizing upon critical events, again gained control of City Hall. Completing the cycle, popular dissatisfaction with Republican policies, including the closing down of all gambling operations, led to a new era of Democratic domination. Having looked at mass responses to gambling, corruption, and critical events, it is now necessary to consider the organizations which brought about reform and to ask why they never were able to sustain it. First, the discussion will focus upon the law-enforcement agencies which harassed the Stern organization and exposed official corruption. Then we will consider the local political organizations which used these exposés to gain political power.

The critical events which have exposed and publicized official corruption in Wincanton have been, without exception, external in origin. When Irv Stern controlled Wincanton's elected officials, neutralization of the city police department was guaranteed by the appointment of corrupt police officials. Honest, proenforcement policemen were either silenced or put in positions where they could do no "harm." When one period of reform came to an end in 1955, for example, the incoming mayor summoned the old chief into his office. "You can stay on as an officer," the mayor said, "but you'll have to go along with my policies regarding gambling." "Mr. Mayor," the chief said, "I'm going to keep on arresting gamblers no matter where you put me." The mayor assigned the former chief to the position of "Keeper of the Lockup," a permanent station in the basement of police headquarters. When reform mayors took office, however, the same law-enforcement apparatus (with changes in a few leadership positions) was successful in driving most gambling and prostitution from the city.

The anticorruption and antiorganized-crime activities of state and federal law-enforcement agencies have been both spectacular and erratic.[16] Agents

---

[16] For an analysis of some of the unique problems involved in securing the conviction of leaders of crime syndicates (as opposed to isolated gamblers), see G. Robert Blakey, "Aspects of the Evidence-Gathering Process in Organized Crime Cases," in President's Commission on Law Enforcement and Administration of Justice, *Task Force Report: Organized Crime* (Washington: Government Printing Office, 1967), pp. 80–106. Problems of inefficiency and lack of cooperation among federal, state, and local law-enforcement agencies are discussed in *Task Force Report: Organized Crime*, p. 20; and Warren Olney, III, "Federal, State, and Local Cooperation in Law Enforcement," in Morris Ploscowe, ed., *Organized Crime and Law Enforcement* (New York: Grosby Press, 1952), pp. 271–308.

of the state's Alcoholic Beverage Commission have regularly acted against liquor violators, arresting any gamblers or prostitutes encountered in the course of raids. A troop of state policemen stationed in suburban Wincanton Hills has been called upon, while reform mayors have controlled Wincanton, to assist in city gambling and prostitution investigations and arrests. When corrupt officials controlled Wincanton and Alsace County, however, the state police were generally inactive. A check of Wincanton newspaper files during one eight-year period of local corruption showed only two state police gambling raids (once when invited into town by local judges and once at the insistence of a reform governor) and ten prostitution arrests.

Interpretations of this inactivity on the part of the state police are varied —records seized from Stern's numbers bank suggested that a few state policemen were being paid off, and one anti-Stern state policeman believes that Stern attempted to have him transferred out of the Wincanton Hills barracks. Other observers regard this inactivity as the product of a "local option" attitude held by many state police officials. While exercising complete police powers in rural areas, they feel that they should enter a *city* only when invited to do so by its judges or police chief. One illustration of this policy is an event which occurred during an election campaign in the 1950s. A few days after spectacular federal raids on Wincanton horse-betting parlors, the governor visited the city. Asked by reporters about the possibility of a state investigation of local conditions, the governor replied, "I'll launch an investigation in Wincanton whenever her mayor or judges ask me to." Republican candidates for judicial office immediately announced that if elected, *they* would begin investigations of Stern's gambling activities. On the following day, the three incumbent (Democratic) judges officially invited the state to investigate at will. (Ensuing prosecutions of Stern and three of his aides, for extorting payments from pinball-machine distributors, collapsed when the complaining witnesses lost interest in testifying, probably after being threatened by Stern agents.)

The role of *federal* enforcement agencies has varied from year to year depending upon what Stern was doing at the time and upon the priorities set by each agency. The Alcohol and Tobacco Tax Division (ATTD) of the Internal Revenue Service has been active in Wincanton since Prohibition, most recently, in 1958, in closing down the Wincanton River distillery.[17] Apart from this activity by the ATTD (and it will be recalled that since Stern

---

[17] For a description of the role of ATTD in combating organized crime, see U.S. House of Representatives, Committee on Government Operations, "The Federal Effort Against Organized Crime," Hearings before the Legal and Monetary Affairs Subcommittee, 90th Cong., 1st sess., 1967, pp. 78ff. (hereinafter cited as "The Federal Effort").

had no interest in the sale of narcotics, the U.S. Bureau of Narcotics was not active in Wincanton), the chief federal agency working to break up Stern's empire was the Intelligence Division of the Internal Revenue Service, aided in one instance by the Federal Bureau of Investigation and, after 1961, by the Organized Crime and Racketeering Section (OCRS) of the Department of Justice.[18] The Intelligence Division was interested in Wincanton for a variety of reasons, including possible violations of laws governing coin-operated gambling devices,[19] persons engaged in the business of accepting wagers,[20] the 10-percent excise tax on wagers received,[21] and income tax on all income whether derived from lawful business enterprises or from illegal activities such as vice, gambling, extortion, kickbacks, etc.[22] Evidence gained during a grand jury investigation of income-tax violations led to indictments on charges of extortion in interstate commerce.[23] As a result of newspaper coverage of the 1956 dispute over pinball machines (following which Stern's nephew was retained as a "public relations man"), the Intelligence Division began to look more closely at Wincanton and seized forty-four pinball machines which lacked the $250 federal gambling-device stamp. Pinball distributors quickly purchased stamps, and Intelligence sought another mechanism for acting against Stern. After two years of investigation, Intelligence agents raided Stern's numbers bank, but were unable to secure evidence directly tying Stern to its operations. Finally, in 1961, Intelligence was able to secure a conviction against Stern for failing to pay excise taxes on numbers receipts, leading to a prison sentence of four years and a $35,000 fine against Stern, as well as lesser sentences for seven subordinates.

Imprisoning Stern, Intelligence quickly discovered, had little impact on the scale of gambling activities in Wincanton. Appeals to the United States Supreme Court dragged on for two years, subordinates carried on the numbers, dice, and horse-betting operations, and local officials continued to protect them. Shortly after Stern's conviction, however, concern was developing in Washington over the growth of organized crime throughout the nation, and Attorney General Robert F. Kennedy increased the staff and activities of

---

[18] For the history and structure of OCRS and the Intelligence Division of the Internal Revenue Service, see "The Federal Effort," pp. 10ff. and 60ff.; *Task Force Report; Organized Crime*, pp. 10–12; and U.S. House of Representatives, Committee on Government Operations, "Federal Effort against Organized Crime: Report of Agency Operations," 90th Cong., 2nd sess., 1968.

[19] 26 U.S.C. 4461–4463.

[20] 26 U.S.C. 4411–4423. The requirement that persons who accept wagers register with the government and purchase an occupational stamp was ruled in 1968 to be a violation of the Fifth Amendment's protection against self-incrimination. See *Marchetti* v. *United States*, 88 S.Ct. 697 (1968) and *Grosso* v. *United States*, 88 S.Ct. 709 (1968).

[21] 26 U.S.C. 4401–4405.

[22] 26 U.S.C. 1–1501 (subtitle A).

[23] 18 U.S.C. 1951–1952. For a complete listing of the laws enforced by the OCRS, see "The Federal Effort," pp. 34–35.

the Organized Crime and Racketeering Section in the Department of Justice. With limited manpower and resources, OCRS leaders concluded that concentration on a few target areas would produce more dramatic results than a "shotgun" approach.[24] Since the Intelligence Division had already acquired substantial information about Stern's operations, Wincanton was chosen as one of the first target areas for OCRS. Information collected by Intelligence about the dice game was given to the F.B.I.; this led to a raid in 1962 and the conviction of many of its operators. While Intelligence continued its surveillance of numbers and lotteries (leading to further convictions of Stern and his associates in 1964), OCRS opened grand jury investigations of corruption on the part of city officials. Since extortion, bribery, etc., are primarily state offenses, the only *federal* charges which OCRS was able to pin on city officials involved extortion in interstate commerce. In 1963 indictments were brought against Stern and Mayor Walasek involving kickbacks from out-of-state firms which sold parking meters to the city. Conviction of both men in 1964 brought low penalties (each received a thirty-day jail sentence), but the attendant publicity led to the election of a reform mayor and district attorney who, using *state* gambling and extortion laws, were able to complete the destruction of Stern's organization.

Reform Movements in Wincanton Politics

> The Alsace Independent Democrats could go out today and get 6,000 votes if we had to. This is the figure that we have maintained since about 1962. But this isn't quite enough to carry us through. It is just shy of the necessary amount for victory. If we have a cause, like we have had at times, we can carry the day. But without a cause, our working membership loses enthusiasm and we can't win. Our organization could be a lot more effective if it would learn to negotiate to gain more power; so long as it tries to be only a reform movement, it will have a rough time trying to win elections.
>
> —A leader of the Alsace
> Independent Democrats, 1966

In and of themselves, state and federal investigations and prosecutions only rid Wincanton of a few leaders of the Stern syndicate; as noted by the federal agent quoted at the beginning of this chapter, they did not solve "the political problem." Corrupt city officials continued to tolerate the gambling

---

[24] Cf. Assistant Attorney General Fred M. Vinson, Jr., testifying in 1967 before a Congressional committee: The strategy of OCRS "is to focus and to choose targets in a given area and then to discuss these targets with the investigative agencies in their jurisdictional limits; then to conduct grand juries." See "The Federal Effort," p. 23.

activities carried on by Stern's subordinates. These investigations did, however, serve as critical events, which aroused public interest in corruption and law-enforcement policies. Several possibilities were open to the Wincantonites who wanted to translate this public interest and sense of outrage into a change in official policies. One was to work through community organizations to persuade present city officials to destroy Irv Stern. The other two involved working to elect reform officials, either as Republicans challenging corrupt Democrats, or as a reform faction within the Democratic Party. All three strategies have been used at different times by Wincanton reformers, and an analysis of their successes and failures may indicate both the peculiar qualities of corruption and reform as political issues and the difficulties inherent in sustaining political reform and strict law enforcement.[25]

A number of interest groups and organizations have attempted to bring about reform in Wincanton by harassing city officials. The Chamber of Commerce and the Ministers' Association, for example, frequently called upon the city government to act against the most visible gambling centers and brothels. A few specific demands were met (the police told several club owners and candy-store operators to move slot machines out of the reach of children), but the usual response was false agreement ("But we've *already* ordered the police chief to arrest all gamblers") or helpless sympathy ("We can't send the state police into Wincanton unless the mayor or police chief asks for help"). The Wincanton newspapers had somewhat more success, but only for short periods of time. Articles on local gambling led to the arrest of a few numbers writers, and a series on prostitution (with photographs) caused the county judge to order the closing of the largest brothel in the city. Within a few weeks of the arrests, however, both the numbers writers and the prostitutes were back in business. While the newspapers and business groups constituted a remote threat to city officials with their ability to attract the attention of outsiders (one Internal Revenue Service agent said that this newspaper publicity had aroused federal interest in Wincanton), they posed few electoral dangers, since the voters tended to regard their charges as partisan propaganda for Republican candidates.

The Republican Party has been a more successful vehicle for attacking

---

[25] For a discussion of various types of local reform movements, see James Q. Wilson, "Politics and Reform in American Cities," in Ivan Hinderacker, ed., *American Government Annual, 1962–1963* (New York: Holt, Rinehart and Winston, 1962), pp. 37–52; and James Q. Wilson, *The Amateur Democrat: Club Politics in Three Cities* (Chicago: University of Chicago Press, 1962). The history of recent reform movements in Wincanton is outlined in Clifford L. Karchmer, "Corruption and Reform in [Wincanton]: A Theoretical Study" (Unpublished B.A. thesis, Princeton University, 1968).

official corruption.[26] A minority party since the 1920s, it has had strong financial support from the business community but little voter appeal; most registered Republicans in Alsace County live in the suburbs. Since there have been few rewards (at the local level, at least) for service to the Republican Party, it has been easy for reformers to name the Republican candidates for local office (a caucus of bankers and industrialists often chooses the candidates without a primary battle), but the candidates have seldom won in the general elections. Lacking widespread support, the Republicans have usually campaigned as a single-issue party, reciting the history of Watts-Donnelly-Walasek corruption. Apart from their victories following the critical events of 1951 and 1963, however, this strategy has had little success. The voters have quickly forgotten the corruption of former administrations,[27] and the honesty of Republican mayors has failed to produce an enduring realignment of voter preferences, so the normal Democratic dominance is reinstated as soon as the *short-term* corruption issue (*"this* candidate was a thief"*) disappears.[28]

Because these reform-minded groups and the newspapers have been unable to influence city officeholders (or to dictate who would win office), and because the Republicans have never been able to rise above their minority status for extended periods of time, it is likely that the only prospects for permanent reform lie within the Democratic Party. Since the demise of the local Socialist Party in the 1940s, however, the Democratic Party has been split into a series of warring factions, which have united to defeat Republicans but which have otherwise been unable to form a stable governing coalition. The labor unions and ethnic clubs have produced a number of candidates in each primary election, each with his own neighborhood base of support. The labor unions have been split, with the steelworkers endorsing liberal or reform candidates and the trade unions supporting various "regulars."

The fragmentation of the Wincanton Democratic Party both facilitated the rise of reform factions and limited their chances to establish permanent control of the party. In 1962, during a city controversy over the adoption

---

[26] For a discussion of the role played by minority parties in injecting new issues into political discussions, see Theodore J. Lowi, "Toward Functionalism in Political Science: The Case of Innovation in Party Systems," *American Political Science Review,* LVII (September, 1963), 570–583; and his *At the Pleasure of the Mayor* (New York: Free Press, 1964), chap. 8.

[27] *The American Voter* points out a sharp decline in "corruption" references to the Democratic Party between the 1952 and 1956 surveys: "The swift decline of comment of this sort suggests that mismanagement and corruption are not issues that are easily kept alive after a change in control of the government." See Angus Campbell *et al., The American Voter,* abridged ed. (New York: Wiley, 1964), p. 21.

[28] Cf. the discussion of "deviating," "realigning," and "reinstating" elections in Campbell *et al., op. cit.,* chap. 16.

of the council-manager form of government (which was defeated by a margin of *six* votes in a city-wide referendum), a group called the Alsace Independent Democrats was formed. With a nucleus of former Socialists, ministers, and teachers from a local college and·the city schools, AID was able to elect high school teacher Ian Redford to the State Assembly in 1962, and offered a full slate of candidates in the Democratic primaries of 1963. AID-endorsed men won both races for the city council, but placed second in the mayoral and district attorney contests; all Democratic nominees were defeated in the general elections following the indictments of Stern and Walasek. In the face of criticism from "regulars" that AID attacks in the primaries had led to the Republican victories in 1963, AID leaders became more accommodating, uniting in 1965 to support a councilmen's slate composed of one AID leader and one "regular" from the Polish community. During the 1967 primaries, however, AID rejected demands to unite behind a regular candidate for the mayoral nomination; with the primaries falling two days after the previously noted publication of the *Task Force Report: Organized Crime,* AID candidate Redford narrowly defeated the "regular" candidate and won the general election the following November.

The 1967 elections gave AID a three-to-two majority on the city council, but it has been unable to form a stable governing group. With statutory control over the police department, Redford has continued the strict law-enforcement policies of the Whitton administration, but the AID councilmen have cooperated on little else. Some AID leaders, like the man quoted earlier, want to move away from the reform issue and build stronger ties with the "regulars"; others, including the intellectuals and the former Socialists, want to maintain the organization's doctrinal purity and emphasis on reform and social change.[29] This conflict, unresolved at the time of this study, reflects the constant dilemma of reformers working within the party system. To build a record which will attract enough Democrats to ensure primary victory, they will have to cooperate with the regulars on the council, but cooperation and negotiation may lead to the alienation of the liberals and intellectuals whose activities brought about the original AID victories.[30]

This discussion of corruption as a political issue suggests that it has a predominantly negative quality. Charges of corruption which have been documented and publicized by critical events can destroy candidates, but

---

[29] Despite the repeated success of AID candidates in Democratic primaries, the reform group has gained little power within the party organization. As of 1968, only 25 AID members sat on the 192-member Democratic County Committee, although an additional 50 committeemen supported an AID candidate for county chairman. Since the county committee does not endorse candidates in the primary, this low committee representation has not greatly hurt the reformers.

[30] J. Q. Wilson, "Politics and Reform . . . ," p. 44.

honesty (an absence of corruption) will not by itself capture voter attention and enduring support. When voters appraise *honest* officeholders, they think in different terms, acting on the basis of historic party identification, desires to gamble, patronage, petty favors, and so forth. Comments from the 1966 survey about the Republican administration of Ed Whitton indicate the limited extent to which "reform" has satisfied popular demands: "This administration is about average for Wincanton: the streets are dirty and the crime rate is about the same. It's honest but no more efficient than the dishonest one we had before." "We've been Democrats all our lives, but in 1963 I voted against Walasek. As for 1967, I'll have to see who the Democrats put up: if he's a good man, I'll probably vote for him." "The Republicans will be licked in 1967 because they got rid of bingo and increased tax assessments. The poor dumb fools only get in when the Democrats get too corrupt." As sociologist Eric McKitrick has concluded, "A reform government which offers nothing as a substitute for the functions performed by the machine will find itself very shortly in a state of paralysis."[31]

---

[31] Eric L. McKitrick, "The Study of Corruption," *Political Science Quarterly,* LXXII (December, 1957), 508.

chapter six

The Consequences
of Corruption

*If you could ever get the opinion-makers—the newspapers
and the ministers—off the corruption issue, you might have
a civilized election in this town.*
                              —A FORMER WINCANTON MAYOR, 1966

*Crime has not only corrupted American government for its
own purposes; it has also tended to immobilize government
for many other purposes. The problems of the American
city . . . are not going to be solved by the dimwits whose
campaigns are financed by the syndicates. And is there any
reason to suppose that the leaders of organized crime are
incapable of perceiving that they will be better off if American municipal government remains fragmented, unco-ordi-
nated, and in the hands, as much as possible, of incompetents?*   —DANIEL PATRICK MOYNIHAN, 1961[1]

THE corruption which has been documented in the pre-
ceding chapters led to the violation of many city, state, and national laws.
Laws forbidding gambling and prostitution were ignored, city contracts and
licenses were awarded to those willing to pay the highest bribes, city jobs
went only to those who kicked back part of their salaries, and so forth. Were

---

[1] "The Private Government of Crime," *Reporter*, xxv (July 6, 1961), 18.

there *other* consequences of this corruption? Apart from the way in which criminal laws and codes of official conduct are administered, does it make any difference whether a government acts honestly or corruptly?[2] Students of other forms of corruption have concluded that it has a number of beneficial, if indirect, effects: it can serve to permit the coexistence of both gambling and moralistic legislation;[3] to overcome the fragmentation of formal authority in government;[4] and to meet the welfare and socialization needs of immigrants in an alien environment.[5] In modernizing areas, corruption has been viewed as a catalyst for inclining political leaders toward economic development, mobilizing the bureaucracy to aid entrepreneurs, and persuading traditional elites to accept economic and social change.[6] Did Wincanton's corruption have similarly beneficial side effects? In the following pages, an attempt will be made to identify both the individuals and organizations immediately affected by corruption, and the long-range impact which it has had upon governmental policies and political processes in Wincanton. Showing causal relationships will be almost impossible (simply to establish that a corrupt city had incompetent leaders or low expenditures does not *prove* that they are related or that one caused the other), but an exploration of these relationships may aid in evaluating the corruption which Wincanton has known.

---

[2] The opportunities and limitations involved in the analysis of the consequences of public policies (using policies as the independent rather than the dependent variables of analysis) are discussed in Austin Ranney, ed., *Political Science and Public Policy* (Chicago: Markham, 1968). See also James W. Davis, Jr., and Kenneth M. Dolbeare, *Little Groups of Neighbors: The Selective Service System* (Chicago: Markham, 1968), pt. 2.

[3] Charles E. Merriam, *Chicago: A More Intimate View of Urban Politics* (New York: Macmillan, 1929); Harold D. Lasswell, "Bribery," *Encyclopedia of the Social Sciences,* II (New York: Macmillan, 1930), 690–692; M. McMullan, "A Theory of Corruption," *Sociological Review,* IX (July, 1961), 181–201; V. O. Key, Jr., "The Techniques of Political Graft in the United States" (Unpublished Ph.D. dissertation, Department of Political Science, University of Chicago, 1934).

[4] Henry Jones Ford, "Municipal Corruption," *Political Science Quarterly,* XIX (December, 1904), 673–686; James Q. Wilson, "Corruption: The Shame of the States," *The Public Interest,* No. 2 (Winter, 1966), 28–38.

[5] Key, "Techniques of Political Graft in the United States."

[6] Nathaniel N. Leff, for example, argues that graft "can induce the government to take a more favorable view of activities that would further economic growth" and "provide the direct incentive necessary to mobilize the bureaucracy for more energetic action on behalf of the entrepreneurs." See "Economic Development through Bureaucratic Corruption," *American Behavioral Scientist,* VIII (November, 1964), 10. See also McMullan, *op. cit.;* and Ronald Wraith and Edgar Simkins, *Corruption in Developing Countries* (New York: Norton, 1964). J. S. Nye, however, argues that "it is probable that the costs of corruption in less developed countries will exceed its benefits except for top level corruption involving modern inducements and marginal deviations and except for situations where corruption provides the only solution to an important obstacle to development." See "Corruption and Political Development: A Cost-Benefit Analysis," *American Political Science Review,* LXI (June, 1967), 427. See also Colin Leys, "What is the Problem about Corruption?" *Journal of Modern African Studies,* III (August, 1965), 215–230.

The Beneficiaries of Nonenforcement of Gambling Laws

> I feel as though I am sending Santa Claus to jail. Although this man dealt in gambling devices, it appears that he is a religious man having no bad habits and is an unmeasurably charitable man.
>
> —A federal judge sentencing slot-machine distributor Klaus Braun to jail in 1948

> When I was a kid, the man in the corner grocery wrote numbers. His salary was about $20 a week and he made $25 more on book.
>
> —A candidate for the Wincanton City Council, 1963

Who benefited when the Wincanton police ignored organized gambling? Irv Stern, of course, made a great deal of money from his gambling operations; federal agents believe that he deposited several millions of dollars in numbered Swiss bank accounts. Wincantonites also believe that a number of local politicians have been well rewarded while in office—that Gene Donnelly and Bob Walasek, each of whom was raised in the slums of Wincanton, collected at least a quarter of a million dollars in payoffs from Stern. (Walasek, however, claimed to be penniless when ordered to pay a fine in 1964.) Apart from the gamblers and politicians and the occasional bettor who beat the odds and won more than he lost, the major beneficiaries of gambling were the organizations which relied upon slot machines and bingo to finance their activities, the businesses which accepted bets as a sideline, and the hotels, bars, and restaurants which catered to the gambling trade. Few estimates of their numbers are available (a very rough guess might be that several hundred persons operated the various forms of gambling, five to ten thousand people gambled in one way or another, and a hundred or so profited from the existence of gambling without being directly involved in it), but the following illustrations may be suggestive.

The social life of Wincanton is organized around clubs, lodges, and other voluntary associations. Labor unions have union halls; businessmen have luncheon groups, country clubs, and service organizations such as Rotary, Kiwanis, the Lions, etc. Each nationality group has its own meetinghouse —the Ancient Order of Hibernians, the Liederkranz, the Colored Political Club, the Cristoforo Colombo Society, etc. In each neighborhood, a P.T.A.-type group is organized around the local playground. Each fire hall is the nightly gathering place of a volunteer firemen's association. Each church has the usual assortment of men's, women's, and children's groups. For many of those organizations, gambling was an indispensable means of attracting members and paying bills; thriving when the police tolerated gambling, some organizations were forced to close their doors following periodic crackdowns.

The interest which these organizations had in police enforcement policies was revealed during a conflict over slot machines in the late 1940s. A newly elected district attorney announced on taking office that slot machines were illegal. With the help of the state police and county detectives, he began to seize slot machines in the rural parts of Alsace County. Following local custom, however, he turned to the mayor and city police to act against slot machines within Wincanton city limits. Mayor Jim Watts took a halfway position; while ordering the police to confiscate any slot machines found in public places, he declared that the powers of the city police did not extend to gambling in "private clubs conducted for the benefit of their own members."

Watts' announcement produced a mixed reaction. The clubs, of course, were overjoyed; the slot machines were vital money-makers for clubs with few members or members who were unwilling to pay high annual dues. Indeed, the slot machines had frequently led to the clubs' coming into existence. Stern and Braun often agreed to finance the purchase or remodeling of club buildings simply in return for freedom to install slot machines in them. The privileged status conferred on the clubs by the mayor's declaration of powerlessness was immediately protested by the clubs' competitors, the bars, restaurants, and hotels whose gambling apparatus had been removed pursuant to the district attorney's order. The Retail Liquor Dealers Association publicly complained that continued possession of slot machines was giving the private clubs an unfair advantage in attracting patrons. Under this pressure, the mayor yielded, announcing that police would also act against machines found in private clubs; within a few days, all machines in the city had gone into storage.

Slot machines were unavailable in Wincanton for eleven weeks. In its first issue in 1949, however, the Wincanton *Gazette* proclaimed:

Alsace County greeted 1949 with the ringing of bells . . . and lemons and cherries and oranges and plums. Old Father Time hardly had his bags packed last Friday night when clubs throughout the city and county were reported oiling their uncovered slot machines in preparation for a Merry New Year's Eve business.

From early 1949 until federal investigators came into town two years later, five hundred slot machines continued to enrich both the clubs and Stern and

Braun. The basis for the mayor's new-found tolerance of machines in the private clubs remained a mystery for only a short time, however. Shortly after the machines reappeared, the president of the Volunteer Firemen's Association reported that fire halls had been contacted by representatives of Klaus Braun's syndicate. Fire halls which agreed to purchase $1.25 "Christmas Tree Stamps" for each punchboard lottery, and to contribute 25 percent of their slot-machine revenues to the syndicate, would be guaranteed protection from police harassment. (The fire halls, it might be noted, generally owned their own machines; those clubs which leased machines from Stern or Braun received protection as part of their "lease.") The firemen refused, so far as is known, to buy the stamps or pay for protection, but their immunity continued. While state police and county detectives continued to seize slot machines found in rural areas of the county, the mayor declared that city police would only act against private clubs if citizens complained; he then proceeded to ignore the complaints of the Retail Liquor Dealers Association. One persistent complainant, a restaurant owner active in Republican politics, was harassed by city health inspectors and obscene telephone calls until he threatened to call the newspapers.

The official policy of nonenforcement of gambling laws was thus profitable to many ethnic, political, and firemen's organizations. While seldom displaying slot machines, other city groups took advantage of police leniency, probably without paying for protection. Local playground associations, for example, sponsored bingo games to pay for equipment, Little League uniforms, and so forth, while businessmen used lotteries to advertise "Downtown Wincanton Days." Wincanton churches and charities also benefited, both directly and indirectly, from gambling. Like the other private groups, a number of these churches and charities sponsored bingo, lotteries, etc. In addition, leading gamblers and racketeers have been generous supporters of Wincanton charities. Klaus Braun literally gave away most of his gambling income, aiding churches, hospitals, and the underprivileged. Braun provided 7,000 Christmas turkeys for the poor in 1947, and frequently chartered buses to take slum children to ball games. Braun's Prospect Mountain Park offered free rides and games for local children (while their parents were in other tents patronizing the slot machines). Irv Stern gave a $10,000 stained-glass window to his synagogue, and aided welfare groups and hospitals in Wincanton and other cities. (Since the residents of Wincanton refused to be treated in the room which Stern gave to Community Hospital, it is now used only for the storage of bandages.) When Stern came into federal court in 1961 to be sentenced on tax-evasion charges, he was given character references by Protestant, Catholic, and

Jewish clergy, two hospitals, and a home for the aged. Critics charge that Stern never gave away a dime that wasn't well publicized; nevertheless, his contributions did benefit valued community institutions. (Lest this description be misleading, it should also be stressed that many ministers protested vehemently against gambling and corruption, leading reform movements and launching pulpit tirades against Stern, Walasek, *et al.*)

To conclude this discussion of the beneficiaries of nonenforcement of vice and gambling laws, there was a group of "fringe beneficiaries" whose *legitimate* business increased when vice and gambling laws were ignored by the Wincanton police. Many of the *providers* of gambling, of course, also had legitimate activities; "Mom and Pop" grocery stores often sold bread, milk, and cigarettes to men and women dropping off their bets, and clubs provided drinks and entertainment for their slot-machine and lottery patrons. Examples of *completely* legitimate fringe beneficiaries include the local bus company, which lost business when Mayor Whitton banned bingo in 1964, and the department stores whose gift certificates were awarded as bingo prizes. Several drugstores sold large quantities of cosmetics to local prostitutes.[7] One hotel offered special weekend rates for the gamblers at the dice game, who would gamble at night and sleep during the daytime. Several landlords rented space to Stern for his bookie parlors and accounting offices. One landlord asked, worried that federal investigations might terminate a profitable arrangement, "Who else would pay $150 a month for that basement?" Being the center of gambling and prostitution for a wide area also meant increased business for the city's restaurants, bars, and theaters. One man declared that business at his Main Street restaurant was never as good as when gamblers and bingo players were flocking to the downtown area.[8]

The Beneficiaries of Other Forms of Corruption

We decided to open a new branch of our bank, and needed a traffic light installed. The mayor suggested that the light would be approved more quickly

---

[7] Former Chief Justice Earl Warren once recalled that "while he was a prosecuting attorney, he had tried to close down organized prostitution in his city, but his efforts were strenuously resisted by bankers, real estate dealers, and retail furniture dealers, all of whom increased their profits by dealing with the prostitute organization at rates higher than those available from honest citizens and legitimate organizations" (quoted by Donald R. Cressey in *Theft of the Nation* [New York: Harper & Row, 1969], pp. 61–62). For a general discussion of the similarities and contrasts between "legitimate" and "illegitimate" business practices, see Thomas C. Schelling, "Economic Analysis and Organized Crime," in President's Commission on Law Enforcement and Administration of Justice, *Task Force Report: Organized Crime* (Washington: Government Printing Office, 1967), pp. 114–126.

[8] At some point, vice may become so widespread as to be bad for business. Writing sixty years ago, Robert C. Brooks noted that "cases are by no means uncommon where the better business element has risen in protest against lax and presumably corrupt business methods which permitted vice to flaunt itself so boldly on retail thoroughfares that respectable women became afraid to venture upon them." See *Corruption in American Politics and Life* (New York: Dodd, Mead, 1910), p. 8.

if Architect X drew the plans. His fee was somewhat exorbitant, but we got the job done.   —A Wincanton bank official

We've built municipal water and sewer systems all over the world, and had done a lot of work for Wincanton. When the time came to award the design contract for a new sewage disposal plant, however, the mayor said that Y would have to get a $10,000 "finder's fee." We told him to go to hell. The mayor announced that our firm was "unqualified," and gave the contract to someone else.   —A Wincanton architectural engineer

Chapter Three noted that toleration of gambling was only one of the forms of corruption practiced by Wincanton politicians, although it probably was the most frequent and rewarding. "Free-lance" corruption also had a number of beneficiaries, although it also produced a number of more directly injured "victims" than did the toleration of gambling. The persons affected by this corruption can be ranked in terms of the willingness with which they participated in the corruption and in terms of the illegality of the transaction (apart from the bribe involved). The most innocent were those who were asked to pay for city privileges to which they were legally entitled. Like the bank official quoted above, businessmen submitting routine applications for building permits often received hints from city officials that approval would come more quickly if the application was accompanied by a "political contribution" or if certain architects, contractors, or lawyers were to do the work. At times, as mentioned earlier, applying for a permit became a cat-and-mouse game, with the official waiting to see how much would be offered, and the applicant waiting to see if he could get his permit without paying for it. In one case uncovered by a reform district attorney, a desperate businessman paid $750 for a permit after his application had lain on an official's desk for three months. Other men, however, said that they received their permits simply by waiting or threatening to call the papers. Where time was important, however, many businessmen considered a $25 or $50 bribe the lesser of two evils.

A more typical participant in official corruption was less innocent, either personally initiating discussions of payoffs or else liberally inflating a contract price in order to cover the bribe. A few examples will suggest the extent to which this type of participant was actively involved in the process of corruption.

—In beginning negotiations for a city purchase of 1,500 parking meters in 1960, Mayor Walasek reminded the salesman that "it costs a lot of money to become a mayor. I'd like to get at least $12 per meter." Hardly shocked, the salesman responded with a counteroffer of $7.50. "I don't think

I can get $12 out of my company. There isn't as much money in meters as there used to be." Irv Stern, fearing that Walasek would mess up everything, forced both men to agree to a bribe of $10 a meter. The obvious willingness of the salesman to pay off led a federal judge (trying Stern and Walasek on charges of extortion) to conclude that the salesman should have been on trial as well. "Those in business, the sanctimonious businessmen who pointed fingers of guilt at others, should have sentence imposed on them, and not walk out as free men," the judge said.

—A salesman of fire trucks was called into the mayor's office and asked if he wished to make a contribution to the Democratic Party. The salesman asked how much was expected. "Since the contract is for $80,000," the mayor was reported to have said, "I think $2,000 would be the right amount." After checking with his company, the salesman delivered $2,000 to a designated city councilman. Although no evidence was ever found that the money reached the Democratic Party treasury, a judge refused to conclude that extortion was involved; the salesman freely admitted that the only "threat" present was the loss of a sale if the money wasn't paid.

—A developer renting a large tract of land from the city sought to purchase it. City officials agreed on a sale price of $22,500, with a like amount being quietly distributed among the officials. A few years later, the land was resold for over $100,000.

—To secure a city contract involving an architect's fee of $225,000, one corporation presented a "finder's fee" of $10,700 to an associate of Bob Walasek and Irv Stern.

In all of these transactions, the city received an acceptable result (new parking meters or firetrucks, architect's drawings, etc.) at the cost of inflated prices covering the bribes and kickbacks. In a third set of cases, however, the beneficiaries of corruption secured favors of more questionable value. The operator of a burlesque show, for example, paid at least $25 per week to escape the demands of local clergymen that the show be closed under the state obscenity laws. One real estate developer secured a zoning variance to erect a high-rise apartment building in a single-family residential area, while another arranged for the construction of a shopping center in an area zoned for industrial uses; both men are believed to have paid off city officials before the variances were approved.

In comparison with the number of beneficiaries of nonenforcement of gambling laws, probably far fewer people benefited from the other forms of corruption taking place in Wincanton, and even within the city's business community there was an uneven distribution of profit from official corruption. For some businessmen, corruption presented opportunities to increase sales and profits. If minor building-code violations could be overlooked, houses and office buildings could be erected more cheaply. Zoning variances, secured for a price, opened up new areas in which developers could build. In selling to the city, businessmen could increase profits either by selling inferior goods or by charging high prices on standard goods when bidding was rigged or avoided.

Finally, corruptible officials could aid profits simply by speeding up decisions on city contracts, or by forcing rapid turnover of city-owned curb space through either "10-minute parking" signs or strict enforcement of parking laws. (Owners of *large* stores, however, sought to maximize profits by asking the police to *ignore* parking violations, feeling that customers who worried about their meters would be less likely to stay and buy.)

While corruption aided some businessmen, many Wincanton businessmen were injured by the Stern-Donnelly-Walasek method of operations and fought vigorously against it. Most leaders of the Wincanton business community—bankers, industrialists, the Chamber of Commerce, etc.—fought Walasek and Stern, refusing to kick back on anything, and regularly called upon state and federal agencies to investigate local corruption. In fact, official corruption affected businesses in different ways. Businesses whose markets lay primarily outide the city usually had only to fear that the mayor might force them to pay for building permits. Companies dealing with City Hall, however, were exposed to every extortionate demand that the mayor might impose; agencies usually able to underbid their competitors were ignored if they refused to abide by the unofficial "conditions" added to contracts. Businesses with a local clientele but no government contracts were in an intermediate position, both in terms of their freedom to act against the system and in terms of the impact which it had upon them. Like the others, they suffered when forced to pay for permits or variances. Legitimate businesses, such as liquor stores, taverns, and restaurants, whose functions paralleled those of the clubs, lost revenue when the clubs were permitted to have gambling and slot machines. Those businesses, such as banks, whose success depended upon community growth suffered when the community's reputation for corruption and gambling drove away potential investors and developers. (Interestingly, businessmen disagree as to whether it is the reputation for corruption or for gambling which discourages new industry. Several Wincanton bankers stated that no investor would run the risk of having to bribe officials to have building plans approved, permits issued, and so forth. One architect, however, argued that businessmen *assume* municipal corruption, but won't move into a "sin town"—their employees will not want to raise children in such surroundings.)

A final aspect of gambling and corruption seems trivial in comparison with the factors already mentioned, but it was cited by most of the business leaders interviewed. Simply stated, it was embarrassing to have one's home town known throughout the country for its vice and corruption. "I'd go to a convention on the West Coast," one manufacturer recalled, "and everyone I'd meet would say, 'You're from Wincanton? Boy, have I heard stories about that place!' I would try to talk about textiles or opportunities for industrial development, but they'd keep asking about the girls and the gambling." A housewife in her fifties recalled, "Things were so bad [under Mayor Walasek] that you even hated to tell people where you were from. Stern and Walasek gave us a bad reputation." Another housewife apologized after detailing to an interviewer the history of local corruption. "Ain't it awful the way we talk about our city? But honest to God, people move away from here and are ashamed to tell where they are from."

The Indirect Consequences of Corruption. For each of the individuals and organizations discussed thus far, corruption has had an immediate and tangible meaning—"This city contract was won (or lost) because of a bribe," "One-half of our club's revenues came from slot machines or bingo," "I had to pay $25 to get my building permit," and so forth. It is also likely, although the evidence is less clear, that Wincanton's long history of corruption has affected more basic characteristics of the Wincanton political system—the recruitment of city officials and employees, the policies followed by the city government, and the attitudes of city residents. Consideration of these long-range consequences of corruption, however, will require an expansion of the terms on which corruption is evaluated. Even if it is felt that the *short-term* benefits of corruption (satisfying the desires of those who wish to gamble or visit prostitutes, adding to the revenues of stores and restaurants, making possible the survival of marginal businesses and social clubs, and so forth) outweigh the costs (law violations, uneconomic use of funds by gamblers or by the city to cover the cost of payoffs, prolonged survival of obsolete businesses such as "Mom and Pop" stores, etc.), it must be asked whether the short-term net benefits of corruption outweigh its long-range costs. Answers to this question require a number of assumptions as to what recruitment, governmental programs, and citizen attitudes *should* be, but it would appear that Moynihan is correct in asserting that corruption and organized crime can immobilize government far beyond issues of law enforcement.

The process of political recruitment has been affected by corruption in many ways. While there have been surprisingly few charges of election fraud in Wincanton, perhaps because of the use of voting machines and the supervision of elections by county judges, syndicate money has frequently affected elections by giving some candidates the opportunity to "treat" supporters in the neighborhood clubs (see Chapter Two) and to buy radio and television time during campaigns. Syndicate money and the patronage available at City Hall also made it possible to reward faithful party workers after the campaign was over.[9] Over the years, corruption (or the *issue* of corruption) probably has affected both the type of men who have sought public office and the platforms on which they have run. Simply stated, the history of corruption in Wincanton City Hall has dissuaded competent and energetic men from running for office or working for the city. With the exception of one Socialist mayor during the 1930s, Wincantonites feel that most of their city officials have been of mediocre ability, whether they were honest or corrupt; a few have lived up to Moynihan's definition of "dimwits." A few innovative civil servants (particularly in the fields of planning and urban renewal) have been brought in from other cities, but low salaries and the general practice of rewarding political supporters has meant that there are few rewards for city employees who excel or innovate;[10] it is assumed that every new administration will reorganize city departments to reward their friends. Thus Mayor Walasek's shuffling of the police department after he took office was unusual only in that some new officials had to pay for their jobs, not in the extent of reorganization or the demotion of incumbent department leaders.

This explanation of official mediocrity should not be carried too far, of course, since many factors besides corruption would tend to discourage competent leaders from seeking local office. Salaries have been low (the mayor received $9,500 when this study was conducted, the councilmen $8,500), the commission form of government has required the mayor to share power with councilmen who have almost total autonomy in operating their own de-

---

[9] On the value of corruption in sustaining party activists when other incentives are unavailable or ineffective, see Edward C. Banfield, *Political Influence: A New Theory of Urban Politics* (New York: Free Press, 1961), p. 257; V. O. Key, Jr., "Techniques of Political Graft"; Fred W. Riggs, "Bureaucrats and Political Development: A Paradoxical View," in Joseph LaPalombara, ed., *Bureaucracy and Political Development* (Princeton: Princeton University Press, 1963). For a general discussion of the role of underworld money in election campaigns, see Alexander Heard, *The Costs of Democracy: Financing American Political Campaigns,* abridged ed. (Garden City, N.Y.: Doubleday, 1960), pp. 135–147.

[10] See Nye, *op. cit.*

partments,[11] and city positions have seldom proved stepping-stones to higher office (since 1945, only Mayor Donnelly was able to win an election—to the state legislature—after serving as mayor). Given the undesirability of the office, it is perhaps not too surprising that weak or temptable men have constituted the majority of local office-seekers, but the tainted image of City Hall has not aided in bringing forth more capable men.

Reinforcing the low caliber of city officials in immobilizing the Wincanton government has been the impact of corruption on the content of political debate and governmental programs. Since the major variation among Wincanton officials has been whether they were honest or corrupt, not whether they responded significantly to urban problems, the issue of corruption has followed a Gresham's Law, driving other issues out of electoral discussion. Should Democratic candidates try to shift the subject to other issues, the Republicans and the Republican-oriented newspapers drag out the history of Democratic thievery and obscure Democratic officials' performances in other areas. While no one can be sure that Wincanton voters would have supported more issue-oriented candidates if they had not been desensitized by forty years of corruption, the former mayor quoted at the beginning of this chapter is probably correct in stating that the issue of corruption has made it impossible to hold "a civilized election" in Wincanton. As James Q. Wilson has noted with reference to official corruption in New York City, "Whatever was good or bad about the official—however competent or incompetent he had been in the conduct of public affairs, however profound or superficial in the analysis of the city's problems—all that was in large measure obscured by the fact, real or imagined, that public power had been used for private purposes."[12]

The same problem of "which comes first" limits analysis of the impact of corruption on the programs which have been adopted by the Wincanton government. In Tables 2.1 and 2.2, it was seen that Wincanton consistently taxes and spends less than other cities with similar social and economic characteristics, ranking *last* in the state in the average ratio of observed to estimated performance on taxation and expenditure policies. Many other factors, of course, have contributed to the depressed level of these policies. The fragmentation of the city's governmental structure and political processes has

---

[11] Leaders *interested* in innovation might, of course, have overcome this fragmentation by bribing other officeholders to accept their programs, but few Wincanton officials have been interested enough in change or skillful enough in the uses of either legitimate or illegitimate power to do so. See Ford, *op. cit.,* and Banfield, *Political Influence.*

[12] James Q. Wilson, "Corruption Is Not Always Scandalous," *New York Times Magazine,* April 28, 1968.

tended to reinforce the status quo and retard movements for change,[13] and since most of the service-demanding upper-middle classes[14] live in the suburbs, Wincanton may in fact have fewer people who demand a high level of public services than similar cities have. But just as corruption may have made the voters suspicious of candidates who promise new programs, may it not also have reduced popular willingness to support new programs through higher taxes? Many people feel that a city-wide referendum in 1962 to establish a council-manager form of government (which lost by a margin of *six* votes!) was defeated because of fears that a corrupt politician would be given the powerful position of city manager, and thus have greater opportunity to do harm (even though reformers had hoped the plan would *reduce* corruption). It is impossible to say whether Wincanton would have had more expansive and expensive programs if its officials had not been corrupt, but the data in Tables 2.1 and 2.2 leave open the possibility that corruption has reduced the capacity of the government to act on basic revenue and expenditure problems.

Why? The most enduring and damaging consequence of political corruption has been its weakening of public support for local government. It is difficult to make reliable comparisons with other cities, but responses from the 1966 survey suggest that the residents of Wincanton have little interest in local politics, feel their government has done a poor job, and are suspicious of local politicians and officials. The lack of interest in local affairs is suggested by responses to a question in the 1966 survey. When asked about "local politics, the things that the city government does here in Wincanton," only 9 percent said that they were "extremely interested" in local politics; 13 percent were "quite interested," 40 percent "moderately interested," and 38 percent said that they were "not much interested at all."[15] Only 30 percent

---

[13] See Ranney, *Political Science and Public Policy,* pp. 161–162; and David B. Truman, *The Governmental Process: Political Interest and Public Opinion* (New York: Knopf, 1951)..

[14] See James Q. Wilson and Edward C. Banfield, "Public-Regardingness as a Value Premise in Voting Behavior," *American Political Science Review,* LVIII (December, 1964), 876–887.

[15] Lest this disinterest be thought solely a product of the mediocre performance of Wincanton officials, we might briefly note the findings of studies done elsewhere. M. Kent Jennings, asking a nationwide sample of 1,700 high school seniors which events they followed most closely, found that national affairs were most closely followed (44 percent), followed by international (39 percent), local (11 percent), and state affairs (6 percent). See "Pre-Adult Orientations to Multiple Systems of Government," *Midwest Journal of Political Science,* XI (August, 1967), 291–317. Belknap and Smuckler, however, interviewing residents of a middle-sized Michigan city, found that national problems were felt to be most serious, but that local problems were regarded as more interesting and received more of the respondents' attention. See George Belknap and Ralph Smuckler, "Political Power Relations in a Mid-West City," *Public Opinion Quarterly,* XX (Spring, 1956), 78–81. See also Kenneth P. Adler and Davis Bobrow, "Interest and Influence in Foreign Affairs," *Public Opinion Quarterly,* XXIX (Spring, 1965), 89–101; and Henry Schmandt and William Standing, "Citizen Images of the Fox River Valley," Wisconsin Survey Research Laboratory, Report FV–1 (November, 1962).

thought that the reform government of Ed Whitton was doing a "good" job, 49 percent thought it was "average," and the rest thought it was "poor" or didn't know.

Other questions in the 1966 survey indicate that Wincantonites are rather cynical[16] about politics and politicians. Forty-four percent of the 180 respondents agreed with the statement that "Most politicians in Wincanton take their orders from a few big men behind the scenes whom the public never really knows" (69 percent of these cited racketeers as the "big men"; 22 percent cited businessmen), 32 percent were undecided, and 21 percent disagreed. They had less cabalistic views of state and national politics: only 26 percent thought "this kind of thing" happened in the state capitol, and 33 percent thought it happened in Washington. Politicians were held in low esteem. Fifty-two percent of the respondents disagreed with the statement, "After politicians are elected to office in Wincanton, they usually keep their promises"; 58 percent felt that "Politicians spend most of their time getting re-elected or reappointed." Similar attitudes appeared in other responses. One manufacturer assumed that "the politicians in other cities are better—more aggressive and honest—and want to do more for the people of the city," while a young housewife thought that other cities might have "an idealism that I don't think we have here." A high school teacher added, "There was the crime problem here—that's all people thought about. They were suspicious of the mayor, the district attorney—that was always on the minds of the people." Finally, one young housewife, a newcomer to the city, added, "Where I come from, no politician has ever gone to jail, we've had no madames; somehow they don't quite know what they're doing here. I'm so disgusted with this city and its politics that I don't think I'll ever register or vote."

Should we conclude that these cynical statements were *caused* by Wincanton's history of corruption? Edgar Litt, after studying over five hundred middle-class residents of Boston, concluded that "when a control for age is maintained, a belief in the perfidy of Boston politicians is strengthened by residence in the city and exposure to its political climate."[17] In Chapter Four it was noted that long-term residents of Wincanton were more likely than newcomers to assume official corruptibility (Table 4.6) and were less tolerant of corruption (Table 4.14). Does long residence produce cynism toward politics? Table 6.1 gives some support to Litt's conclusion. Long-term resi-

---

[16] Political cynicism is discussed, using slightly different survey instruments, in Robert E. Agger, Marshall N. Goldstein, and Stanley A. Pearl, "Political Cynicism: Measurement and Meaning," *Journal of Politics,* xxiii (August, 1961), 477–506; and Edgar Litt, "Political Cynicism and Political Futility," *Journal of Politics,* xxv (May, 1964), 312–323.

[17] Litt, *op. cit.,* p. 316.

TABLE 6.1 *High Cynicism, by Age and Percentage of Life in Wincanton*

Percentage of Life in Wincanton	Age						Total	
	21–32		33–59		60 and over			
	%	N	%	N	%	N	%	N
Less than 40%	36	14	43	14	83	6	47	34
40–79%	*	2	63	16	53	32	54	50
80% or more	56	25	59	51	47	19	56	95
Total	46	41	57	81	56	57	54	179

This table shows the percentage of persons in each category who were highly cynical (a score of 3 or 4 on the Cynicism Index described in Chapter Four, note 14). Thirty-six percent of the young newcomers, for example, were highly cynical. Pooling chi-squares between cynicism and residence in the three age categories produced a chi-square of 9.50; with six degrees of freedom, it was significant at the .20 level. The Kendall's tau correlations between cynicism and residence in the three age categories were .23, .13, and −.17. Where less than five cases appeared in a cell, an asterisk (*) was substituted for the percentage figure.

dents are slightly more cynical than those who have lived elsewhere, although among the older residents, the relationship is reversed. The slightly lower cynicism of the older long-term residents may be derived from their introduction to political life during the city's Socialist days, now fondly recalled as having produced the best mayors in the city's history. It might be noted that the most distinct break occurs between those who have been in the city less than 40 percent of their lives and the other respondents. After the initial shock of comparing Wincanton political styles with those of former cities, the respondents seem to level off and even mellow slightly in their opinions of politicians.

Conclusions. What difference has it made that Wincanton has been corrupt for most of the last fifty years? On the positive side, it must be admitted that illegal gambling kept alive many private clubs and social organizations, and supplemented the income of a number of marginal shopkeepers. Short-term costs of illegal gambling and corruption include the law violations themselves (if the act of gambling is regarded as a cost), inflated prices paid on city contracts, bribes paid by businessmen to secure legitimate services, and so forth. The long-range, less measurable costs of corruption have included a loss of trust in politicians and respect for the performance of local government, leading to the recruitment of less competent officials and the depression of most municipal revenue and expenditure policies.

Sixty-five years ago, Henry Jones Ford argued that

It is better that government and social activity should go on in any way than that they should not go on at all. Slackness and decay are more dangerous to a nation than corruption. . . . The graft system is bad, but it is better for a city government to lend itself to the forces of progress even through corrupt inducements than to toss the management of affairs out upon the goose-common of ignorance and incapacity, however honest. Reform which arrests the progress of the community will not be tolerated long by an American city.[18]

True enough. The reformers who have put an end to law-enforcement corruption in Wincanton have generally contributed little else to "the progress of the community." One minister in Wincanton stated the problem neatly: "The Democratic Party often furnishes more creative leadership than the Republican Party does. The housing authority was started by them, and the downtown parking problem was solved, but they were corrupt. The most important thing the Republicans have done is to furnish honest government." But in the long run, the corrupters and corruptees—the Irv Sterns, Gene Donnellys, and Bob Walaseks—have retarded progress more than they have assisted it. The wide-open gambling and the free-lance corruption of the Donnellys and Walaseks have made it harder, not easier, to recruit new industries and investors to replace the declining or departing corporations which built the city at the turn of the century. Progress-oriented officials *could* have used corruption to persuade city councilmen, zoning officials, etc., to acquiesce in projects which might rejuvenate the city, but the more typical pattern has been a conspiratorial sharing of graft for its own sake. Since the areas of Wincanton, as in other metropolitan areas, which are most appealing to industrial developers are the undeveloped suburbs and farmlands, not the decayed, congested, and fragmented parcels of the central city,[19] official corruption has reinforced investors' decisions not to build within city limits. More importantly, as argued by Moynihan earlier, corruption by organized crime has staffed Wincanton City Hall with a series of "incompetents" and "dimwits," men with neither the leadership ability nor the inclination to solve the city's problems of decline and decay. The fact that laws against gambling were not enforced was therefore one of the least significant consequences of corruption; corruption has immobilized the Wincanton political system for other purposes as well.

---

[18] Ford, *op. cit.,* pp. 678, 682–683. See also Robert K. Merton, *Social Theory and Social Structure,* rev. ed. (New York: Free Press, 1957), p. 81; and the works cited in note 6, *supra.*

[19] See John F. Kain, "The Distribution and Movement of Jobs and Industry," in James Q. Wilson, ed., *The Metropolitan Enigma: Inquiries into the Nature and Dimensions of America's "Urban Crisis"* (Cambridge: Harvard University Press, 1968), pp. 2–39.

chapter seven

Law-Enforcement Corruption: Explanations and Recommendations

> *Corruption is . . . limited by the extent to which a sense of outrage is aroused among people who are capable of making corruption more costly than correctness.*
>
> —ROGOW AND LASSWELL, 1963[1]

CORRUPTION is a persistent and practically ubiquitous aspect of political society; it is unlikely that any reforms will ever eliminate it completely. Wherever men compete for valuable but limited commodities, whether they are licenses to operate taxicabs, franchises to sell goods to the government, or freedom to operate a numbers game, there will be a temptation to secure these commodities through corrupt inducements if other efforts fail. Barring some apocalyptic change in human nature, there will always be people who want to gamble, visit prostitutes, or enrich themselves through illegal deals with the government. And, on the other hand, in any large organization, whether it be a police department, tax-collection agency, labor union, or multimillion-dollar corporation, there will always be individuals

---

[1] Arnold A. Rogow and Harold D. Lasswell, *Power, Corruption, and Rectitude* (Englewood Cliffs, N.J.: Prentice-Hall, 1963), p. 74.

who will find the rewards of corruption greater than the satisfactions of legitimate behavior.

If this is correct, then the relevant question becomes one of finding ways to *reduce,* not eliminate, the frequency of corruption—to minimize the situations in which corruption is the rule rather than the exception, situations in which corruption affects not only isolated governmental decisions but also the nature and functioning of the political system. While it might also be desirable to eliminate the petty as well as the most blatant forms of corruption, it would probably be impossible to do this without significantly altering our concepts of civil liberties and of public bureaucracies drawn from and responsive to the general citizenry. Before suggesting a series of actions which might serve to reduce the incidence of widespread corruption, it is necessary to identify precisely those conditions which tend to produce or facilitate it. Some relate more directly to Wincanton and the law-enforcement corruption which has been studied here; others deal more broadly with the general phenomenon of political corruption.

The first precondition for corruption is a substantial conflict over the goals of the legal system. As McMullan notes,

> A high level of corruption is the result of a wide divergence between the attitudes, aims, and methods of the government of a country and those of the society in which they operate. . . . Therefore the different levels of corruption in different countries depend on the extent to which government and society are homogeneous.[2]

A major source of this kind of norm conflict in mid-twentieth-century America concerns legislation which attempts to restrict what is regarded as "immoral" behavior—gambling, prostitution, and the use of narcotics. In Chapter Four, for example, it was noted that one-half of the Wincanton survey respondents felt that "most" or "a lot" of local residents liked to gamble (Table 4.3). Furthermore, 55 percent felt that the state should legalize gambling; between one-third and one-half of the respondents in surveys conducted in other areas shared this opinion.[3] (It should be noted at this point that it is *conflict* over legislation rather than lack of support for it which is necessary for corruption. If officials in cities where *everyone* wanted to gamble tried to exact payments for protection, they would be ousted by local voters.)[4] Thus in Wincanton, as in most heterogeneous cities, there are demands

---

[2] M. McMullan, "A Theory of Corruption," *Sociological Review,* IX (July, 1961), 184–185.
[3] See Table 4.8 and the surveys cited in Chapter Four, note 20.
[4] See James Q. Wilson, *Varieties of Police Behavior: The Management of Law and Order in Eight Communities* (Cambridge: Harvard University Press, 1968), pp. 148–149.

for both the enforcement of the state's gambling laws and the toleration of petty gambling activities; those who wish to gamble will support the syndicates, and the moralists will demand that the town be "kept clean."

Assuming that wherever a substantial demand for illegal goods and services is found,[5] someone will be willing to satisfy it, the next precondition for corruption is a willingness on the part of the relevant governmental agency to tolerate this activity in return for an appropriate payoff. Three factors appear to affect the likelihood that the agency will be so disposed: the internal characteristics of the agency, the characteristics of the political system in which the agency operates (including both the formal governmental institutions and informal groups and processes), and the laws and law-enforcement agencies available for the detection and harassment of corrupt officials and their corrupters.

The internal characteristics of governmental agencies which are most likely to affect their susceptibility to corruption are the strength of organizational leadership, the rewards given for legitimate behavior (pay scales, job security, opportunities for advancement, etc.), and the degree of identification with professional standards and codes of ethics. Where leadership is weak, senior members of the organization will be unable to control members of the organization tempted by bribes. Where rewards given for noncorrupt behavior are low, the relative value of corrupt inducements increases. Where professional identification is low or nonexistent, codes of conduct promulgated by professional organizations will present few psychological barriers to the acceptance of bribes.

On all three counts, the internal characteristics of the Wincanton Police Department have facilitated both toleration of gambling and the acceptance of bribes. (It should be kept in mind, however, that even at the height of the Stern syndicate's activities, probably not more than 10 percent of the force was receiving regular payoffs, although perhaps one-half might have accepted Christmas turkeys or liquor.) Since political involvement in police affairs has been a long-standing tradition in Wincanton—incoming mayors regularly elevate patrolmen to command positions and reduce former chiefs to walking a beat—few police officers have felt free to take full command of their department by harassing lazy or corrupt men on the force. While research was being conducted during the summer of 1966, eighteen months be-

---

[5] National Crime Commission estimates of the volume of illegal gambling suggest that crime syndicates probably have gross revenues from gambling up to $50 billion, with net revenues of $6 or $7 billion per year. See President's Commission on Law Enforcement and Administration of Justice, *Task Force Report: Organized Crime* (Washington: Government Printing Office, 1967), pp. 2–5, and Donald R. Cressey, *Theft of the Nation* (New York: Harper & Row, 1969), chap. 5.

fore a new administration would take office, police officers reported that men on the force were beginning to curry favor with local politicians and that sergeants were becoming unwilling to enforce departmental regulations. "How can I tell someone off?" a captain asked. "If the Democrats take office again, I'll probably be walking a beat and *he* may be my boss!" Given the insecurity of their positions, it is not surprising that few Wincanton police chiefs have been strong leaders; the corrupt ones have been kept busy stealing while they had the chance, and the honest ones have been kept busy trying to hold the force together in the face of persistent political interference and departmental factionalism.

From the point of view of patrolmen on the Wincanton police force, neither the city nor the department have offered high rewards for noncorrupt behavior. During the 1950s, Wincanton police salaries were in the lowest quartile of middle-sized cities in the nation, well below the city's median family income ($5,453); in the 1960s, the salary for patrolmen rose to $5,400, still well below the national average. While the state civil service law guarantees that policemen may not be discharged from the force without cause, only friends of politicians seem to get promotions and desirable duties. Until reform mayor Ed Whitton instituted a series of competitive examinations in 1964, there was little incentive for patrolmen to "hustle." Hustlers were only rewarded if they also had political connections, and those who made enemies (of politicians or of policemen or city officials on Stern's payroll) were likely to find themselves transferred to "Siberia"—dragging drunks out of bars or patrolling the riverfront on the midnight shift.[6] Thus the reward system of the Wincanton Police Department not only offered few incentives for legitimate behavior but also worked against those who refused to "mind their own business." Even for men not on Irv Stern's payroll, "looking the other way" was a clearly advantageous policy.

Finally, there is the matter of "professionalism"—that combination of special training and education which gives men unique competence, adherence to a clear code of ethics, and supervision by a professional association. As has been noted by Wilson, Niederhoffer, and Banton, few policemen in America meet these tests; they learn most of their skills on the job, have few clear standards specifying appropriate behavior, and act collectively through union-like bargaining groups, not professional accrediting associations.[7]

---

[6] Lincoln Steffens observed a similar phenomenon within the New York Police Department while Theodore Roosevelt served as Police Commissioner. Even the policemen who shared his reform values were afraid to act, fearing retaliation when Tammany Hall returned to power. *Autobiography* (New York: Harcourt, Brace, 1931), pp. 275–281.

[7] See J. Q. Wilson, *Varieties of Police Behavior*, pp. 29–30; Arthur Niederhoffer, *Behind the Shield: The Police in Urban Society* (Garden City, N.Y.: Doubleday, 1967), chap. 1; and Michael Banton, *The Policeman in the Community* (London: Tavistock, 1964), pp. 105–110.

Even when compared with this low national standard of professionalism, Wincanton police perform poorly. Until reformer Whitton took office in 1964, no member of the force had attended the F.B.I. National Academy; formal training was limited to a few weeks of classes conducted by senior members of the force. Until Whitton instituted competitive promotional examinations, advancement was based more on friendship with officers and politicians than on abstract skill or merit. Finally, because of repeated political meddling in departmental affairs and public assumptions of police misconduct (only 11 percent of the survey respondents felt that no policemen would take a bribe), departmental morale and *esprit de corps* have been low.[8] A committee of experts asked by the Wincanton government in 1967 to evaluate the department concluded that it represented the "residual remains of temerity, habit, and limited imagination or fear. . . . Their general morale is low, and their pride, if any exists, is well hidden." Under these conditions, it is not surprising that professionalism has not served as a significant barrier to corruption within the Wincanton police department.

The second broad set of factors which will influence the likelihood that a governmental agency will be corrupt, beyond the internal characteristics of the agency itself, is the nature of the political system in which it operates: the interests and values of the citizenry, the structure of governmental agencies, the activities of political parties and interest groups, and so forth. If most residents are unaware of governmental policies or positively desire illegal goods and services, then the agency will be free to adopt tolerant or corrupt policies. If neither government officials nor private organizations have the ability or desire to demand official morality, then the agencies will be free to act as they please. If, on the other hand, officials, political parties, or private elites are capable of establishing control over the political process, governmental agencies will more likely be forced to accede to their demands. (That an official is powerful does not, of course, necessarily mean that he will be honest or interested in strict law enforcement. Only powerful men, however, will be *able* to supervise bureaucratic activities and, to the extent that they view entreaties from corrupters as threats to their own control over their organizations, they will be likely to want to end corruption or centralize it under themselves.)[9]

Chapters Four and Six suggested a number of ways in which the attitudes

---

[8] See also James Q. Wilson, "Police Morale, Reform, and Citizen Respect: The Chicago Case," in David J. Bordua, ed., *The Police: Six Sociological Essays* (New York: Wiley, 1967), pp. 137–162.

[9] See Daniel P. Moynihan, "The Private Government of Crime," *The Reporter,* xxv (July 6, 1961), 14–20; James Q. Wilson: "Corruption Is Not Always Scandalous," *New York Times Magazine,* April 28, 1968; and *Varieties of Police Behavior,* pp. 148–149.

of Wincanton residents have facilitated the growth of corruption in law-enforcement agencies. In addition to being sharply divided over the value of antigambling legislation, the survey respondents had little interest in city politics and were poorly informed about the government and its law-enforcement agencies. As one real estate broker put it, "Walasek stole darn near everything he could put his hands on. It was made easy for him because most of the city residents didn't pay attention and just went along with it." Even though they were cynical about politicians and were hostile to corruption, the survey respondents were slow to assume that corruption might be involved in city affairs or that corruption might soon return to the city. When asked in 1966 what issues would be important in the 1967 local elections, only nine of the 180 respondents felt that "clean government" or keeping out vice and gambling might be an issue (55 percent had no opinion, 15 percent felt that the recent ban on bingo might be an issue, and 12 percent cited urban renewal, a subject frequently mentioned in the papers in the months preceding the survey). Since, under Ed Whitton, the city was being honestly run and was free from gambling and prostitution, there was no "problem" to worry about. To the extent that they were interested in local politics, it was in terms of issues which affected them personally ("The Republicans increased my property assessment"; "My wife can't play bingo now"; "We need a new playground in the neighborhood"); to the extent that they were interested in the activities of the police department, it was in terms of protection against violence, not the enforcement of morals legislation.

To what extent are the public institutions and private political groups of Wincanton capable of dealing with threats of subversion by crime syndicates? In Chapters Two and Six, it was noted that the formal governmental structure of the city is exceedingly fragmented. Although he can name the officers of the police department, the mayor has little control over either city councilmen and their departments or the independently elected district attorney who handles all criminal prosecutions. The county's political parties, as noted in Chapter Five, are also fragmented organizations which exercise little or no control over city officials; candidates for local office develop their own *ad hominem* coalitions. The city's business community, while probably influential in many recent urban renewal and economic development decisions, has been unable to dominate other aspects of city politics, including the selection of city officials, for at least forty years.[10] While the Wincanton newspapers regularly attacked organized crime, they were never able by themselves to provoke voter rebellions against official corruption; until state

---

[10] For discussions of historical changes in the role of economic dominants in urban politics, see the works cited in Chapter Two, note 9.

and federal investigators provided proof of the corruption underlying local gambling, the papers were forced to concentrate on the gambling itself, hardly a startling or offensive subject for most Wincantonites. As a result of this fragmentation of the formal and informal political processes of Wincanton, it might be said that the city knew a "power vacuum," a situation in which *no one* was able to dominate local politics or to control the Stern syndicates and its corrupt officials. Unlike the old-time bosses who were powerful enough to keep gamblers and prostitutes within limits, Wincanton officials usually took orders from the Stern syndicate. With no one dominating the city's political system, it was easy for Stern to name his own terms, fearing only the intervention of state or federal investigators.[11]

The final factor which affects the likelihood that corruption will develop within a political system concerns the laws and the law-enforcement agencies which are available for the investigation and harassment of corrupt officials. In many areas of American politics, the laws defining corrupt behavior are quite ambiguous: campaign contributions by government contractors are permissible, but *quid pro quo* payments to secure a particular contract are not; contributions to legislators prior to the adoption of a law are frequently legitimate, but contributions to the policemen who administer the law never are.[12] In general, however, the kinds of cash transactions seen in Wincanton which were payments to secure a contract or protection from the police are clear violations of state and local laws, although this may be difficult to prove in court. There are greater variations among cities and among states in the level of investigations and prosecution of official corruption. In some areas, city, state, and federal agencies are constantly scrutinizing official behavior, either in conjunction with an interest in specific programs (e.g., a road-building program or the collection of taxes) or as part of an interest in official morality for its own sake. Wincanton presents a rather mixed picture: federal investigators, particularly from the Internal Revenue Service and the Department of Justice, have been very interested in organized crime in Wincanton but have been only peripherally interested in official corruption; state agents, on the other hand, have stayed out of the city unless officially invited to act. District attorneys and county judges have taken a similarly passive stance, processing those cases which the police have brought to them, but only rarely (twice during the Donnelly-Walasek era) initiating independent

---

[11] That corruption is most likely to develop in political systems which are unable to handle current societal problems is suggested by James C. Scott, "An Essay on the Political Functions of Corruption," *Asian Studies*, v (December, 1967), 501–523; and Samuel P. Huntington, "Political Development and Political Decay," *World Politics*, xvii (April, 1965), 386–430.

[12] See Scott, *op. cit.*, and Herbert E. Alexander and Laura L. Denny, *Regulation of Political Finance* (Berkeley: Institute of Governmental Studies, and Princeton: Citizens' Research Foundation, 1966).

investigations. Apart from federal agents, therefore, Irv Stern had little to fear so long as he could buy protection from Wincanton officials and police-men. If other agencies had taken a more independent view of their role in law enforcement, Stern's tenure in Wincanton would have been of much shorter duration.

Proposals for Change. Can anything be done to minimize widespread corruption? The feasibility of change depends on the extent to which reforms would require the acquiescence of large numbers of people who are committed to the present state of affairs. Edelman and Fleming, after studying European programs to preserve wage-price stability, concluded that indirect actions (changing bank interest rates, reserve requirements, or currency values) were more successful than actions requiring changes in public attitudes or habits: "No democratic government can for long enforce behavior which is strongly resisted by the public, so that when the pressure of public opinion is lacking, enforcement is likely to be absent too, regardless of formal law or declared public policy."[13] If this is correct, then the only feasible paths for reducing corruption are changes which are consistent with existing public attitudes or changes which will work primarily through government officials and law-enforcement agencies without requiring changes in mass behavior patterns. Nothing will significantly reduce popular desires to gamble or make corrupt deals, but the following suggestions may reduce the attractiveness of corruption by increasing the capacity of government to deal with it.

First, law-enforcement corruption might be reduced by improving the internal structure of law-enforcement agencies. While it may be desirable, if difficult, to improve police efficiency through the recruitment of better officers and the expansion of training programs,[14] the primary changes needed in cities like Wincanton concern job security and protection against "political interference." With higher salaries, promotions through competitive examinations, and civil service protection for ranking officers, a police department could both increase loyalty to the organization (offering psychological defenses against the temptations of corruption) and reduce the ability of corrupt politicians to arrange police toleration of organized crime. It is unlikely that even the most drastic increases in salaries or job security will *eliminate*

---

[13] Murray Edelman and R. W. Fleming, *The Politics of Wage-Price Decisions: A Four-Country Analysis* (Urbana: University of Illinois Press, 1965), pp. 317–318.

[14] See, generally, the recommendations of the President's Commission on Law Enforcement and Administration of Justice, *Task Force Report: The Police* (Washington: Government Printing Office, 1967).

the sense of isolation and frustration felt by American police,[15] but changes in this direction might produce a greater sense of professionalism and freedom from local politicians. Although such changes would also, of course, reduce the ability of honest and progressive local officials to alter police policies, they may be necessary to strengthen those agencies which have the greatest exposure to corruption.

The second step for increasing resistance to corruption concerns the role of state and federal enforcement agencies. As has been seen in Wincanton, some state police units take a hands-off attitude toward local crime and corruption problems, while others conserve limited resources by concentrating only on selected target areas. While they have steadily escalated the scope of their attack on gambling, narcotics, and the other business activities of the syndicates, federal agents have seldom been able to act against official corruption, since bribery and extortion involving local officials (unless they affect interstate commerce) are not federal offenses.[16] In many cases, law-enforcement agencies are so suspicious of each other (often correctly assuming that some agents in other organizations are on the payroll of the syndicates) and jealous of their agency's prestige (wanting to reserve the "big pinch" for themselves) that they refuse to cooperate with each other. The results of this conflict have been both a fragmentation of the skills devoted to the problem of organized crime and the reduction of that check on corruption which would result from separate organizations looking for syndicate collusion with police and city officials.[17]

The recommendations which have been made thus far are designed to increase the scope and efficiency of official actions against organized crime and to create incentives within police departments to avoid corruption. As indicated earlier, corruption can also be facilitated by certain weaknesses of local political systems—mass apathy or contempt for the government, the inability of local officials to control enforcement agencies, and the absence of private organizations (political parties, interest groups, citizen associations) which could structure the political process and fill the "power vacuum"

---

[15] See, for example, James Q. Wilson: "The Police and their Problems: A Theory," *Public Policy*, XII (1963), 189–216; and "Police Morale . . . ."

[16] In a message to Congress in 1969, President Nixon proposed laws making the corruption of local officials and policemen a federal offense, subjecting both corrupters and corruptees to fines and jail sentences. See *New York Times*, April 24, 1969.

[17] To overcome the inertia caused by corrupt local police and to remedy other problems in the prosecution of syndicate members, the National Crime Commission recommended the annual impaneling of investigative grand juries with special prosecuting and investigative staffs, provision for the granting of immunity to witnesses, and the power to impose extended sentences on syndicate leaders. Furthermore, the commission called for the formation or expansion of special organized crime units in federal, state, and local law-enforcement agencies, and the development of information-sharing facilities. See *Task Force Report: Organized Crime*, pp. 16–22.

which allows a crime syndicate to become the most active force. How might this be accomplished? The most likely source of such a strengthening of the local political system would be an expansion of the powers of the mayor. If Wincanton, for example, adopted a mayor-council structure to replace the commission form of government, more qualified (and publicly attractive) men might find the office worth seeking, and the mayor would have greater ability to oversee the police department and to institute programs which might restore citizen interest in local government and support for its programs.[18] To increase the tax resources for such programs and the involvement of enforcement- and program-oriented middle classes in city affairs, some form of metropolitan area-wide government may be necessary.[19] Many of the most exciting and interest-attracting programs for the cities are, of course, financed by federal grants; to reward local officials who reduce corruption, and to convince voters that reform officials can provide more than their own honesty, federal officials might consider a policy of giving urban renewal and Model Cities grants to cities which have successfully reformed. If the legitimate rewards of public office increased (both through increases in salaries and powers and through the satisfactions of major improvements in declining cities), energetic men might be more willing to seek public office, and the focus of political discourse might shift from the issue of corruption to more pressing urban issues. If local government became a more promising vehicle for local action (and less tainted by corruption), it is likely that private interest groups and political organizations would increase their interest in municipal affairs. As the visibility of governmental activities increased, citizen support might increase, and suspicious official behavior would be more quickly noticed. Citizen crime councils, so long as they did not simply harass policemen and reduce morale, might serve as an appropriate vehicle for public interest in crime and law-enforcement problems. Improvement of the activities of local political parties would require an increase in the availability of legitimate funds,[20] but it might be hoped that an improvement in govern-

---

[18] That mayors with greater formal authority and party support are more capable of implementing unpopular decisions is argued by Robert L. Crain, Elihu Katz, and Donald B. Rosenthal. See *The Politics of Community Conflict: The Fluoridation Decision* (Indianapolis: Bobbs-Merrill, 1969). See also J. David Greenstone and Paul E. Peterson, "Reformers, Machines, and the War on Poverty," in James Q. Wilson, ed., *City Politics and Public Policy* (New York: Wiley, 1968), pp. 267–292; Robert L. Crain and James J. Vanecko, "Elite Influence in School Desegregation," in Wilson, *City Politics and Public Policy*, pp. 127–148; Edward C. Banfield and James Q. Wilson, *City Politics* (Cambridge: Harvard University Press, 1963), chaps. 8 and 11.

[19] For a comprehensive review of various forms of metropolitan government, see John C. Bollens and Henry J. Schmandt, *The Metropolis: Its People, Politics, and Economic Life* (New York: Harper & Row, 1965).

[20] See Edward C. Banfield, *Political Influence: A New Theory of Urban Politics* (New York: Free Press, 1961), pp. 256–257; Moynihan, *op. cit.*

mental performance would increase mass willingness to contribute time and money to the parties and to run for local office.

Finally, corruption might be minimized by a reduction in the conflict between popular values and formal legislation. In recent years, two broad strategies have been proposed to meet this problem. One calls for an increase in law-enforcement activity, coupled with an educational campaign designed to inform the public of the relationship between consumption of illicit goods and services and the growth of organized crime and corruption.[21] The other strategy assumes that an irreducible mass desire to gamble should be accommodated through the legalization of gambling and/or the operation of gambling activities by the government.[22] Both proposals agree that the public is inadequately aware of the problems of organized crime and corruption, and that popular apathy and desire to gamble have encouraged the growth of corruption. Both probably would agree on the need for a uniform set of policies on a statewide or, optimally, nationwide basis. Where gambling is legal in some areas but illegal in others, it is easy for the syndicates to use the former locations as bases for operations in the latter.[23] They disagree, however, on the consequences of legalization. The proponents argue that once gambling was legalized, police corruption would cease. The opponents argue that legalization would increase the number of gamblers and would simply deflect the syndicates into other areas of illegal activity in which they would be equally corruptive; because of the skills required to operate large-scale gambling activities, syndicate leaders would quickly take control of legalized gambling unless it was operated directly by the government. Criminologist Donald R. Cressey has argued that the insatiable greed of the syndicates demands some form of calculated appeasement, such as negotiations leading to

---

[21] See Virgil W. Peterson, *Barbarians in Our Midst: A History of Chicago Crime and Politics* (Boston: Little, Brown, 1952), pp. 331–333; Morris Ploscowe, "New Approaches to the Control of Organized Crime," *Annals of the American Academy of Political and Social Science,* CCCXLVII (May, 1963), 74–81; Eliot H. Lumbard, "Local and State Action Against Organized Crime," *Annals of the American Academy of Political and Social Science,* CCCXLVII (May, 1963), 82–92. The role of the syndicates in operating gambling casinos in Nevada is discussed in Wallace Turner, *Gamblers' Money: The New Force in American Life* (Boston: Houghton Mifflin, 1965).

[22] Among those endorsing the legalization of gambling, with or without government operation, are Jerome H. Skolnick, "Coercion to Virtue," *Southern California Law Review,* XLI (1968), 588–641; John M. Murtagh, "Gambling and Police Corruption," *Atlantic Monthly,* CCVI (November, 1960), 49–53; Sanford H. Kadish, "The Crisis of Overcriminalization," *Annals of the American Academy of Political and Social Science,* CCCLXXIV (November, 1967), 157–170; National Council on Crime and Delinquency, *Goals and Recommendations: A Response to "The Challenge of Crime in a Free Society"* (New York: National Council on Crime and Delinquency, 1967); Robert K. Woetzel, "An Overview of Organized Crime: Mores versus Morality," *Annals of the American Academy of Political and Social Science,* CCCXLVII (May, 1963), 1–11.

[23] See *Task Force Report: Organized Crime,* p. 11.

syndicate control of gambling in return for an end to syndicate violence, corruption, and other unlawful activities.[24]

This study has offered but little information on which to base a choice between these proposals. Surveys show a substantial popular desire to gamble, one which might be reduced (but scarcely eliminated) by a strict enforcement policy or increased by easily available legitimate gambling opportunities. Many Americans have an equally intense belief that gambling is wasteful or sinful; they regard proposals to legalize gambling as a threat to government's symbolic role as the protector of public morality.[25] It is true that intermittent reform movements in Wincanton have been able to reduce greatly the level of gambling and corruption in the city. On the other hand, legalization would reduce the incentive to corruption, freeing police resources for other purposes and giving the police a more popularly accepted set of laws to enforce. Would the syndicates simply move into other equally illegal and equally corrupting activities? I don't know. To the extent that there is greater (but hardly unanimous) public support for police action against the kinds of activities to which the syndicates might turn (e.g., the sale of narcotics, loan-sharking, labor racketeering), the dangers of corruption would be less than in the case of gambling. It is clear, however, that the situation in cities like Wincanton, where long periods of massive corruption are only intermittently disturbed by short periods of honest but otherwise ineffectual reform, is intolerable.

---

[24] Cressey, *Theft of the Nation,* chap. 12.
[25] Edelman and Fleming, *op. cit.;* Murray Edelman, *The Symbolic Uses of Politics* (Urbana: University of Illinois Press, 1964).

Appendix A

THE 1966 ATTITUDE SURVEY

1. Selection of the Sample. The population sampled consisted of all adults (aged twenty-one or over) residing within the city limits of Wincanton. A random sample of 392 addresses was drawn from the 1965 City Directory. From each sample address which contained eligible respondents, a respondent was selected for interviewing, using the Kish[1] procedure for objective respondent selection.

2. The Survey Process. Interviews were conducted by eight trained female interviewers from the Wisconsin Survey Research Laboratory under the direction of Professor Harry Sharp. Interviews took place in the respondents' homes, and in most cases lasted between thirty minutes and two hours. As it was known in advance that a nationwide television program during the survey period would discuss organized crime, and as it was believed that a substantial portion of the program would deal specifically with Wincanton, the sample of addresses was randomly divided into two parts of approximately equal size. One part was subjected to field processing during the seven days prior to the television program; following the program, processing of the first subsample was discontinued and the second subsample was put into the field. (The responses of the two subsamples are compared in Chapter Four, note 9.)

3. Response Rate. A sample of 392 addresses was sent into the field. The results of the field operation for the two subsamples and the combined sample are summarized in Tables A.1 and A.2.

---

[1] Leslie Kish, "A Procedure for Objective Respondent Selection Within the Household," *Journal of the American Statistical Association,* XLIV (September, 1949), 380–387.

TABLE A.1 *Classification of Addresses into Nonsample and Eligible Categories for the Two Subsamples*

	Total Number of Addresses	Nonsample	Eligible Addresses
Subsample I	192	20	172
Subsample II	200	29	171
Total	392	49	343

TABLE A.2 *Classification of Eligible Sample Addresses into Response and Nonresponse Categories by Percentage*

	Subsample I		Subsample II	Total
Completed interviews	48%		57%	52%
Nonresponse	52		43	48
Refusals		20%	23	22
Not at home		23	9	17
Respondent away		2	5	3
Unable to participate		1	5	3
Not processed		6	—	3
Total	100%		100%	100%
Total number of eligible addresses .	172		171	343

From the combined sample of 392 addresses, 343 addresses containing eligible respondents were obtained. These 343 addresses yielded 180 completed interviews giving the study an overall response rate of 52 percent.

Processing the first subsample of 192 addresses yielded 172 addresses containing eligible respondents; twenty addresses were nonsample, i.e., did not contain eligible respondents. Some examples of nonsample addresses are business establishments, parks, schools, churches, etc. The nonsample addresses were visited by an interviewer to verify that no one lived at the address in question. Eighty-two completed interviews were obtained from the 172 eligible addresses, a response rate of 48 percent. Except for 11 addresses, all 172 addresses received at least one call from an interviewer. The results of these calls are shown in Table A.2.

Processing of the second subsample of 200 addresses yielded 171 eligible addresses, which in turn yielded 98 completed interviews. The percentage of eligible addresses yielding completed interviews is, therefore, 57 percent. In this phase of the study, at least three calls were made at each address. The results of these calls are summarized in Table A.2.

Five nonresponse categories are used in Table A.2. An address is classi-

fied as a "refusal" if the respondent refused to be interviewed. The "respondent away" classification is used if the respondent is out of town for the
duration of the study, e.g., on vacation. Addresses are placed in the "not-at-
home" category if the respondent is never at home when the interviewer
calls. If the respondent is contacted and available for an interview, but because of some barrier cannot be interviewed (e.g., the respondent might be
sick, senile, or unable to speak English), the address is placed in the "un-
able-to-participate" category. Finally, we include a category for those addresses where no calls were made.

4. Comparison of the Sample and the Population. In Table A.3, the 180
survey respondents are compared with the city's 1960 population in terms
of education, sex, race, income, and age. Generally speaking, the sample is
overrepresentative of the better-educated and of women; it is also slightly
overrepresentative of nonwhites, the elderly, and persons with incomes over
$10,000.

TABLE A.3 *Comparison of 1966 Survey Respondents with 1960 City Population*

Classification	Population	Sample
1. *Education*		
	1960 Population (Persons 25 yrs. of age and over)	**1966 Sample (180 persons 22 yrs. of age and over)**
Elementary		
0 thru 4 yrs.	9.0%	7.2%
5 thru 7 yrs.	23.0	12.2
8 years	20.1	11.1
High school		
1 thru 3 yrs.	21.2	30.6
4 years	18.7	24.4
College		
1 thru 3 yrs.	4.1	7.8
4 or more yrs.	3.9	6.1
Not ascertained	0.0	0.6
Total	100.0%	100.0%
2. *Sex*		
	1960 Population (Persons 21 yrs. of age and older)	**1966 Sample (180 persons 22 yrs. of age and older)**
Male	46.5%	38.3%
Female	53.5	61.7
Total	100.0%	100.0%

TABLE A.3 (*cont.*)

Classification	Population	Sample
3. *Race*		
	1960 Population (Persons 20 yrs. of age and older)	**1966 Sample (180 persons 22 yrs. of age and older)**
White	96.7%	92.8%
Nonwhite	3.3	7.2
Total	100.0%	100.0%
4. *Income*		
	1960 Population (Families)	**1966 Sample (180 persons and families)**
Less than $3,000	18.0%	23.9%
$ 3,000–$ 4,999	25.5	20.0
5,000– 6,999	27.0	23.3
7,000– 9,999	19.0	17.2
10,000– 14,999	8.1	8.9
$15,000 and over	2.4	3.9
Not ascertained	—	2.8
Total	100.0%	100.0%
5. *Age*		
	1960 Population (Persons 21 yrs. of age and older)	**1966 Sample (180 persons 22 yrs. of age and older)**
21–29	14.4%	16.1%
30–39	17.9	20.6
40–49	20.0	15.6
50–59	18.9	16.1
60–69	15.8	14.4
70 and over	12.9	17.2
Total	99.9%	100.0%

5. Content of the Questionnaire. The questions asked of the survey respondents, modified so as to disguise the names of the city and of individuals, are as follows (background questions dealing with the respondent's occupation, political beliefs, etc., have been omitted):

1. We're interested in talking to Wincanton area people on a variety of topics. First, on the subject of *local* politics . . . the things that the city government does here in Wincanton . . . are you extremely interested in local politics, quite interested, only moderately interested, or not much interested at all?

2. In your opinion, is the present city government in Wincanton doing a very good job, a good job, about average, a poor job, or a very poor job?

3. Why do you feel this way?
4. We're interested in what the city government does for the local citizens. What things does the city do that are most important to you? (Anything else?)
5. Over the last twenty years, what mayor of Wincanton has done the best job in providing the services that are most important to you?
6. Some people say that the city government does too much, and others say that it doesn't do enough. How about you . . . what things—if any—does the city government do now that you would like to see it stop doing?
7. What things—if any—is the Wincanton city government *not* doing now that you would like to see it *start* doing?
8. Suppose the Wincanton city government were considering a regulation or action which you considered unjust or harmful. What do you think you could do?
9. Do you live in the city of Wincanton?
10. In 1962 there was a referendum to set up a council-manager form of government in Wincanton. In that referendum did you vote not to change the form of government, or did you vote to adopt a council-manager form, or didn't you vote?
11. If this referendum were brought up again, how would you vote now?
12. Turning to the 1963 local elections in Wincanton . . . how interested were you in the 1963 contest for mayor; were you extremely interested, quite interested, only moderately interested, or not much interested at all?
13. Did you vote in the 1963 election for mayor?
    13a. Did you vote for (the Republican) or for (the Democrat)?
14. What major issues were there in the 1963 campaign for mayor of Wincanton?
15. Did you vote in the primary elections in 1963? For whom?
16. Did you vote in the 1965 elections for city council? For whom?
17. In next year's city election for mayor, do you think you'll vote for a Republican or a Democrat? Why?
18. Can you think of any issues which may be important in the 1967 local elections? (What are these? Any others?)
    I'll read some things that people can do to help a party or candidate win an election. Please tell me if you did any of these things during *either the 1963 election for mayor or the 1965 election for city council in Wincanton.*

19. Did you talk to any people or try to show them why they should vote for one of the parties or candidates?
20. Did you go to any political meetings, rallies, dinners, or things like that?
21. Did you give any money or buy tickets or anything to help the campaign for one of the parties or candidates?
22. Did you wear a campaign button or put a political sticker on your car?
23. Do you now belong to a political club or organization? Which?
24. Have you ever held an office in a political club or campaign organization? Which office?

    We're interested in what Wincanton residents think or know about certain people. I'll read some names and for each one please tell me who he is or what he does. First . . .
25. (Current mayor) Edward Whitton
26. Irv Stern
27. (Current congressman)
28. (Current district attorney)
29. (Stern lieutenant)
30. (Former chief of police)
31. (Stern lieutenant)
32. (Former mayor) Robert Walasek
33. (Madame)
34. (Former district attorney)
35. (Former federal prosecutor)
36. (Madame)
37. (Former mayor) Eugene Donnelly
38. (Stern lieutenant)
39. (Criminal attorney)
40. (Former city councilman)
41. To your knowledge, has Irv Stern ever been involved in Wincanton politics?

    41a. In what ways and when has he been involved in Wincanton politics?

    Now I'm going to read some statements that you sometimes hear people make. For each statement, please tell me how strongly you agree or disagree with it.
42. First . . . "A good many local elections aren't important enough to bother with."
43. "Public officials don't care much what people like me think."
44. "Voting is the *only* way people like me can have any say about how the city government runs things."

45. "People like me don't have any say about what the city government does."
46. "Sometimes politics and government seem so complicated that a person like me can't really understand what's going on."
47. "To get ahead in the world today you are almost forced to do some things that aren't right."
48. "Every person should give some of his time for the good of his town or city."
49. "Most people are honest chiefly through fear of being caught."
50. "So many other people vote in the national election that it doesn't matter much to me whether I vote or not."
51. "It isn't so important to vote when you know your party doesn't have a chance to win."
52. "If a person doesn't care how an election turns out, he shouldn't vote in it."
53. "There is not much difference between politics in Wincanton and politics in other American cities."
    53a. What differences would you say there are?
54. (Getting back to the agree/disagree statements) "Most politicians in Wincanton take their orders from a few big men behind the scenes whom the public never really knows."
    54a. What kinds of people are these who give the orders? (Any others?) Can you name any of these men?
    54b. Do you think it is a good thing that this happens, doesn't it really matter much, or is it a bad thing?
55. Does this kind of thing happen in the government in (the state capital)?
56. Does this kind of thing happen in Washington?
57. On the agree/disagree statements again . . . "After politicians are elected to office in Wincanton, they usually keep their promises."
58. "Former administrations provided more and better playgrounds for the people of Wincanton than the present administration does."
59. "Underworld elements and racketeers had very little say in what the Wincanton city government did when Mr. Walasek was mayor."
60. "Underworld elements and racketeers have very little say in what the city government in Wincanton does today."
61. "People who are born outside this country should not be allowed to run for public office."
62. "Neighborhoods should be allowed to keep certain people from moving in if they are undesirable."
63. "If a person wanted to make a speech in Wincanton favoring govern-

ment ownership of railroads and big industries, he should be allowed to speak."

64. "If a Communist were elected mayor of Wincanton, the people should *not* allow him to take office."

65. "If a person wanted to make a speech in Wincanton attacking churches and religion, he should be allowed to speak."

66. Turning to another subject . . . England now has legalized the use of narcotics in that drug addicts can get prescriptions for narcotics from doctors. Do you think this idea should be adopted in the United States, or not?

67. Why do you feel this way?

68. The State of New Hampshire recently set up a lottery, and the proceeds are used to support public schools. Do you think (this state) should have a state lottery, or not?

69. Why do you feel this way about a state lottery in (this state)?

70. Some people feel that (this state) should legalize gambling. Others disagree. Do you think this should be done, or not? Why?

71. As you remember it, who was it who decided that bingo should not be played in Wincanton?

72. How do you feel . . . do you think bingo should be allowed here, or not?

73. Why do you feel this way about bingo in Wincanton?

74. If the legislature in (the state capital) does *not* legalize bingo, do you think the mayor and district attorney should continue to enforce the law against bingo, or not?

75. How many of the people in Wincanton like to play bingo . . . would you say most do, a lot, some, or almost none of them?

76. How many of the people in Wincanton like to bet on horse racing . . . would you say most do, a lot, some, or almost none?

77. How many of the people in Wincanton like to play the numbers . . . would you say most do, a lot, some, or almost none?

78. As compared with five years ago, do you think it's easier now, about the same, or harder to place a bet on a horse race in Wincanton?

79. As compared with five years ago, do you think it's easier now, about the same, or harder to find a dice game in Wincanton?

80. Some people say that the present city administration under Mayor Whitton is about the same as when Mayor Walasek was in office. Others disagree. What do you think? Is it about the same or different?

81. Why do you feel this way?

82. How about the district attorney's office . . . do you think that the dis-

trict attorney's office now is about the same as when (the former man) was district attorney, or is it different?

83. Why do you feel this way?

84. Do you think the Wincanton police force now is better, about the same, or worse than it was under Mayor Walasek?

85. Why do you feel this way?

86. As compared to former administrations, is it easier now to talk to people in City Hall, about the same as before, or harder?

87. In 1964, former Mayor Walasek and Irv Stern were convicted of accepting kickbacks on the purchase of parking meters for the city. They were given 30-day jail sentences. Do you feel these sentences were too severe, about right, or too light? Why?

88. During the trial of Walasek and Stern, former Police Chief Phillips testified against them. In your opinion, was it right or wrong for Phillips to testify? Why?

89. Do you think it was right or wrong for the federal government not to prosecute Phillips for his part in the situation? Why?

Now I have a final series of agree/disagree questions.

90. "Churches and other charitable organizations should be allowed to hold bingo games."

91. "Gambling is all right so long as local people, not outsiders, run the game."

92. "No matter what you do, people will always gamble."

93. "Wincanton policemen should be chosen for higher ranks on the basis of civil service examinations, and should keep these ranks even when a new mayor comes into office."

94. "If nobody has been hurt, a policeman should give a speeder a warning instead of a ticket."

95. "The mayor and the police chief should be able to cancel parking and speeding tickets in some cases."

95a. In what kinds of cases should they be able to do this?

96. "Politicians vote for what everyone wants more often than they vote for what just a few people want."

97. "Politicians spend most of their time getting re-elected or reappointed."

98. "It's all right for a city official to accept presents from companies as long as the taxpayers don't suffer."

99. "If a city official takes a bribe to give a contract to somebody, it's more important to prosecute the city official than the man who gives the bribe."

100. "It's all right for the mayor of a city to make a profit when that city buys some land so long as only a fair price is charged."
101. "A city official who receives $10 in cash from a company that does business with the city should *not* be prosecuted."
102. "The Wincanton police today are concentrating on gambling too much."
103. "If there is any gambling going on in Wincanton, it should be handled by local police rather than the F.B.I."
104. "If there is any gambling going on in Wincanton, it should be handled by local police rather than the state police."
105. "No member of the city council would take a bribe, even if he had the chance."
106. "No policeman in Wincanton would take a bribe, even if he had the chance."
107. "No businessman in Wincanton would take a bribe, even if he had the chance."
108. "No official of any local labor union would take a bribe, even if he had the chance."
109. "The police should not break up a friendly poker game even if there is betting."
110. "Burlesque theaters should be closed in Wincanton."
111. "There is way too much obscene literature in Wincanton today."
112. "Mayor Walasek was no different than other Wincanton politicians; he just got caught."
113. "Mayor Walasek did a lot of good for the City of Wincanton."
      113a. What things did Mr. Walasek do that were illegal? (Anything else?)
114. Which of the federal investigative agencies would you say was primarily responsible for most of the prosecutions of Wincanton people in the past ten years?

Appendix B

FACTOR ANALYSIS AND INDEX CONSTRUCTION

In Chapter Four, five indices were used to summarize survey respondents' awareness of and attitudes toward gambling and corruption. In the following pages, I will describe their derivation, component questions, scoring in index construction, and the frequency distribution of scores for the sample of 180 respondents.

1. Information Index. Each respondent was asked to identify ("Could you tell me who he is or what he does?") sixteen persons active in Wincanton politics, crime, or law enforcement; the names are listed above in questions 25–40. When factor-analyzed together with other types of questions, the responses (correct identifications) formed a single factor, with factor loadings of .37 to .80 (with the exception of the name of the federal attorney who prosecuted Irv Stern, all loadings were .52 or higher). When factor-analyzed separately, two factors emerged from the sixteen names, one on which the better-known names (the first seven names in Table 4.1) loaded, and one on which lesser-known names (the last five names in the table) loaded; names in the middle of the table loaded on both factors. Significantly, other factors, such as "criminal names" or "official names," did *not* appear at any time.

A respondent was given two points for each name correctly identified or one point for each name closely identified (e.g., when a man was identified as the state attorney general rather than the United States prosecutor, who had the same name but a different middle initial). For statistical purposes,

Michael R. Kagay of the Department of Political Science, University of Wisconsin, performed the factor analysis and constructed the indices used in this study. Computer time at the University of Wisconsin Computer Center was supported by a grant from the National Science Foundation.

TABLE A.4 *Frequency Distributions on the Information Index*

Score	Number	Percentage
1 (None correct)	8	4%
2–5	13	7
6–10	20	11
11–15	21	12
16–20	21	12
21–25	37	21
26–30	35	19
31–32	14	8
33 (All correct)	11	6
Total	180	100%

one point was added to each respondent's score to eliminate the zero category. The distribution of scores on the Information Index is given in Table A.4.

2. Factor Analysis of Gambling and Corruption Questions. In preliminary tests, twenty-nine questions from the 1966 survey were factor-analyzed[1] to determine whether responses were grouped into dimensions which measured common underlying attitudes. After exclusion of questions which appeared to tap extraneous dimensions or which duplicated other questions, sixteen questions were selected for final factor analysis. Questions 1 through 8 in Table A.5 deal with gambling, while questions 9 through 16 concern bribery and corruption. Questions 1 through 3 and 9 through 12 concern information or awareness of gambling and corruption, while the remaining questions test attitudes toward them. Table A.5 presents the varimax rotated factors of a principal component solution to the problem of what are the factors or dimensions underlying responses to the sixteen questions. With the exception of question 3, we see that the sixteen questions "load on" or are measured by four distinct factors. (The strength of a loading, or degree to which a question "measures" the underlying factor, ranges between −1.00 through .00 to +1.00. The closer the loading comes to −1 or +1, the stronger the association between the question and the factor.)

Since the three questions loading on Factor I deal with perceptions of the popularity of various forms of gambling, we shall call this a Perception of Gambling factor. Questions 4 through 8, loading on Factor II, appear to test attitudes toward gambling, so we shall call this a Tolerance of Gambling factor. Questions 9 through 12 ask whether particular individuals will ac-

---

[1] For an explanation of the theoretical basis and practical applications of factor analysis, see Fred N. Kerlinger, *Foundations of Behavioral Research: Educational and Psychological Inquiry* (New York: Holt, Rinehart and Winston, 1964), chap. 36.

TABLE A.5 *Factor Analysis of Sixteen Gambling and Corruption Questions**

| | Rotated Factor Matrix | | | | |
Question	I	II	III	IV	h^2
1. How many of the people in Wincanton like to bet on horse racing?	**.82**	−.08	.02	.04	.68
2. How many of the people in Wincanton like to play the numbers?	**.86**	−.03	.01	−.10	.74
3. How many of the people in Wincanton like to play bingo?	**.37**	**−.38**	.01	**−.39**	.44
4. Do you think (this state) should have a state lottery, or not?	.10	**−.66**	.03	.14	.46
5. Some people feel that (this state) should legalize gambling. Do you think this should be done, or not?	.18	**−.73**	.04	.12	.58
6. How do you feel . . . do you think bingo should be allowed here, or not?	−.01	**−.74**	.07	−.14	.57
7. Gambling is all right so long as local people, not outsiders, run the game.	.11	**−.74**	.08	−.19	.60
8. The police should not break up a friendly poker game even if there is betting.	−.27	**−.52**	.00	−.08	.35
9. No member of the city council would take a bribe, even if he had the chance.	−.09	.13	**−.84**	−.08	.74
10. No policeman in Wincanton would take a bribe, even if he had the chance.	−.01	.05	**−.90**	−.02	.82
11. No businessman in Wincanton would take a bribe, even if he had the chance.	−.05	−.02	**−.85**	−.18	.76
12. No official of any local labor union would take a bribe, even if he had the chance.	.12	.05	**−.83**	−.21	.75
13. The mayor and the police chief should be able to cancel parking and speeding tickets in some cases.	.06	.06	−.15	**−.61**	.40
14. It's all right for a city official to accept presents from companies as long as the tax-payers don't suffer.	.11	−.24	−.06	**−.60**	.44
15. It's all right for the mayor of a city to make a profit when that city buys some land so long as only a fair price is charged.	−.07	.00	−.02	**−.79**	.64
16. A city official who receives $10 in cash from a company that does business with the city should *not* be prosecuted.	−.03	.03	−.23	**−.73**	.58
Percent of total variance	11	16	19	14	60%
Percent of common variance	18	27	32	24	101%

*The cell entries are factor "loadings" which express the extent to which each question is correlated with one of the underlying factors. Signs show how the question is scored relative to the factor. The communality (h^2) of each question expresses the proportion of the variance of the question that is associated with all four component factors. Loadings greater than .30 are in bold type.

cept bribes, so we shall call Factor III a Perception of Bribability factor. The last four questions concern public policy in situations where corruption may be involved, so Factor IV will be called a Tolerance of Corruption factor. The loading of question 3 on Factors I, II, and IV poses a problem of classification; as we saw in Table 4.3, 88 percent of the respondents felt that "most" or "a lot" of Wincanton residents liked to play bingo, producing a highly skewed distribution of responses to this question. Since the wording of the question specified "how many" rather than "what should we do," it was decided to treat it as an information rather than an attitudinal question, and it is only used in Factor I in the following discussion. (Questions 4 through 16 were also factor-analyzed separately from 1 through 3, and the structure of Factors II, III, and IV remained the same, with only slight variations in the factor loadings.)

3. Perception of Gambling Index. During factor analysis, three questions loaded together on Factor I:

1. "How many of the people in Wincanton would you say like to bet on horse racing? Would you say most do, a lot, some, or almost none of them?"

2. "... like to play bingo?"

3. "... like to play the numbers?"

Since this factor presumably tests the respondents' level of information, a "Don't know" response was regarded as being different in character from any other response, so a respondent giving a "Don't know" response to *any one* of the three questions was given an index score of zero. Other respondents were then given one point for "Almost none" responses, two points for "Some," three points for "A lot," and four points for "Most," producing scores ranging from 3 to 12. Two points were then subtracted from each score to produce an index ranging from 1 to 10. The distribution of scores on the Perception of Gambling Index is given in Table A.6.

4. Tolerance of Gambling Index. During factor analysis, five questions loaded together on Factor II:

1. "The State of New Hampshire recently set up a lottery, and the proceeds are used to support public schools. Do you think (this state) should have a state lottery, or not?"

2. "Some people feel that (this state) should legalize gambling. Others disagree. Do you think this should be done, or not?"

3. "How do you feel? Do you think bingo should be allowed here, or not?"

TABLE A.6 *Frequency Distributions on the Perception of Gambling Index*

Score	Number	Percent
0 (Those who answered "Don't know" to any *one* of the questions)	53	29%
1 (Perception of little gambling)	0	—
2	1	1
3	1	1
4	14	8
5	16	9
6	16	9
7	37	21
8	23	13
9	12	7
10 (Perception of much gambling)	7	4
Total	180	102%

4. "Gambling is all right so long as local people, not outsiders, run the game." (Agree/Disagree)

5. "The police should not break up a friendly poker game even if there is betting." (Agree/Disagree)

In preliminary factor analysis, other presumably similar questions regarding official enforcement of the bingo law or police emphasis on gambling, or regarding burlesque theaters or narcotics, loaded on other, independent factors. Questions dealing with the popularity of bingo and with *church* bingo also loaded with the above five items, but were excluded from the index as they appeared unnecessarily to duplicate question 3; after excluding those items, factor analysis was repeated and the five final items again formed a single dimension.

In scoring the index, respondents were given one point for each "Yes" answer to questions 1 or 2, "Allowed" answer for question 3, or "Agree" answer to questions 4 or 5. This formed an index ranging from 0 to 5; for statistical purposes, one point was added to each score, eliminating the zero category. The distribution of scores on the Tolerance of Gambling Index is given in Table A.7.

5. Perception of Bribability Index. Four questions loaded on Factor III during factor analysis:

1. "No member of the city council would take a bribe, even if he had the chance." (Agree/Disagree)

2. "No policeman in Wincanton . . ." (Agree/Disagree)

TABLE A.7 *Frequency Distributions on the Tolerance of Gambling Index*

Score		Number	Percent
1	(Low tolerance)	18	10%
2		18	10
3		36	20
4		31	17
5		44	24
6	(High tolerance)	33	18
	Total	180	99%

TABLE A.8 *Frequency Distributions on the Perception of Bribability Index*

Score		Number	Percent
1–3	(Perception of low bribability)	3	2%
4–6		8	4
7–9		49	27
10–12		35	19
13–15		75	42
16–17	(Perception of wide-spread bribability)	10	6
	Total	180	100%

3. "No businessman in Wincanton . . ." (Agree/Disagree)

4. "No official of any local labor union . . ." (Agree/Disagree)

Respondents were given one point for "Strongly agree" responses, two points for "Agree," three points for "Undecided" or "Don't know," four points for "Disagree," and five points for "Strongly disagree." Two respondents whose answers to question 1 were not ascertained were scored in the "Undecided" category. This produced an index ranging from 4 to 20; three points were then subtracted to produce an index ranging from 1 to 17. The frequency distribution of scores on the Perception of Bribability Index is shown in Table A.8.

6. Tolerance of Corruption Index. Four items loaded on Factor IV during factor analysis:

1. "The mayor and police chief should be able to cancel parking and speeding tickets in some cases." (Agree/Disagree)

2. "It's all right for a city official to accept presents from companies as long as the taxpayers don't suffer." (Agree/Disagree)

3. "It's all right for the mayor of a city to make a profit when that city buys some land so long as only a fair price is charged." (Agree/Disagree)

TABLE A.9 *Frequency Distributions on the Tolerance of Corruption Index*

Score		Number	Percent
1–3	(Low tolerance)	15	8%
4–6		61	34
7–9		66	37
10–12		31	17
13–15		6	3
16–17	(High tolerance)	1	1
Total		180	100%

4. "A city official who receives $10 in cash from a company that does business with the city should *not* be prosecuted." (Agree/Disagree)

A question testing the perceived popularity of bingo also loaded on this factor (see Table A.5), but was excluded during index construction on the assumption that it tested information rather than attitudes. Respondents were given one point for a response of "Strongly disagree," two points for "Disagree," three points for "Undecided," four points for "Agree," or five points for "Strongly agree." Those who answered "Don't know," and one respondent whose opinions on two of these questions were not ascertained, were scored as "Disagree," the modal category on each question. This scoring produced an index ranging from 4 to 20; three points were then subtracted from each score to produce an index ranging from 1 to 17. The frequency distribution of scores on the Tolerance of Corruption Index is shown in Table A.9.

Appendix C

REGRESSION ANALYSIS OF GOVERNMENTAL POLICIES

In Chapter Two, an attempt was made to see whether major revenue and expenditure policies in Wincanton were significantly different from those in other cities. In comparing Wincanton with the 258 other middle-sized (50,000 to 250,000 population in 1960) cities in the United States, it was necessary first to identify the variables (other than corruption) which were related to each policy. A multiple regression equation estimates, for each set of values for the independent variables, what the value of the dependent variable will be. If we know, for example, that a city had a value of 10 on variable X and 15 on variable Y, the regression equation might tell us to expect a value of 14 on dependent variable Z. The coefficient of multiple determination (R^2) of an equation shows how much of the variation in the dependent variable has been explained; if the R^2 is low, e.g., less than .30, the equation is of little utility in predicting values of the dependent variable. After the regression equation estimates a dependent variable value for a city with specified independent variable values, we can determine whether the city's *actual* (observed) value was above or below the estimated value.[1] The stepwise regression program used in this analysis (the Multiple Linear Regression Program of the Social Systems Research Institute of the University of Wisconsin) first selects that independent variable which shows the highest simple correlation with the dependent variable. In each subsequent step, the program picks up that variable which explains the greatest amount of the as-yet unexplained variation in the dependent variable. In the following paragraphs, we will list the independent variables used in the analysis,

---

[1] For this use of the ratio of observed to estimated values, see Ira Sharkansky, "Economic and Political Correlates of State Government Expenditures: General Tendencies and Deviant Cases," *Midwest Journal of Political Science,* xi (May, 1967), 173–192.

the variables which added at least .01 to the multiple correlation coefficient, and the total R^2 for all variables, corrected for degrees of freedom. With regard to seven other policies, the independent variables failed to explain 30 percent of the variance (an R^2 of .30 or higher), so the policies were not used in the text discussion of Wincanton governmental activities. These variables were: per capita expenditures for sanitation, highways, and health and hospitals; and percentage of municipal budget allocated to fire companies, highways, sanitation, and health and hospitals.

Independent Variables. Twenty-six independent variables were used in the regression program: region (ten sets of states—New England, Border States, etc.); total population; percentage of foreign born; percentage native, of foreign parentage; percentage of persons aged fourteen to seventeen who were in school; median school years completed; nonworker-worker ratio; percentage of females in the labor force; percentage of civilian labor force unemployed; percentage employed in manufacturing industries; percentage employed in white-collar industries; median family income; percentage of families with incomes less than $3,000; percentage of families with incomes greater than $10,000; population per square mile; percentage nonwhite; median age; percentage in same house in 1960 as in 1955; percentage migrant from different county 1955–1960; percentage of housing units overcrowded (with more than 1.01 persons per room); percentage of housing units owner-occupied; form of government; type of election (partisan or nonpartisan); at large vs. ward elections for city council; percentage population change 1950–1960; city age (census year in which the city first reached a population of 25,000).

TABLE A.10 *Per Capita Expenditures on Police*

Variable	Multiple *r*	Increase in *r*
Percentage foreign-born	.4748	.4748
Percentage new to county since 1955	.5755	.1007
Nonworker-worker ratio	.6225	.0470
Percentage with foreign-born parents	.6396	.0170
Percentage overcrowded housing	.6564	.0168

Multiple *r* for 26 Variables = .7460
R^2, corrected for degrees of freedom, = .50

TABLE A.11 *Per Capita General Expenditures*

Variable	Multiple *r*	Increase in *r*
Percentage of housing units owner-occupied	.4087	.4087
Percentage foreign-born	.4626	.0539

TABLE A.11 (cont.)

Variable	Multiple r	Increase in r
Population density	.4945	.0319
Women in labor force	.5236	.0291
Total population	.5433	.0197
Partisan-nonpartisan elections	.5589	.0156
Ward–at-large elections	.5701	.0112
Percentage new to county since 1955	.5829	.0128
Percentage overcrowded housing	.6014	.0185

Multiple r for 26 variables = .6364
R^2, corrected for degrees of freedom, = .34

TABLE A.12 *City Employees per 1,000 Population*

Variable	Multiple r	Increase in r
Percentage of housing units owner-occupied	.5247	.5247
Percentage in new house since 1955	.5649	.0402
Partisan-nonpartisan elections	.5904	.0255
Total population	.6150	.0246
Population density	.6280	.0130
Ward–at-large elections	.6396	.0116

Multiple r for 26 variables = .7147
R^2, corrected for degrees of freedom, = .45

TABLE A.13 *Per Capita Revenue from Taxes*

Variable	Multiple r	Increase in r
Percentage foreign-born	.5946	.5946
Age of city	.6643	.0697
Women in labor force	.6957	.0314

Multiple r for 26 variables = .7871
R^2, corrected for degrees of freedom, = .58

TABLE A.14 *Per Capita General Revenues*

Variable	Multiple r	Increase in r
Percentage of housing units owner-occupied	.4273	.4273
Percentage with foreign-born parents	.5264	.0991
Women in labor force	.5571	.0307
Partisan-nonpartisan elections	.5820	.0249
Total population	.6073	.0253
Population density	.6183	.0110
Percentage new to county since 1955	.6295	.0112
Percentage overcrowded housing	.6476	.0181

Multiple r for 26 variables = .6975
R^2, corrected for degrees of freedom, = .43

TABLE A.15 *Per Capita Expenditures for Fire Protection*

Variable	Multiple *r*	Increase in *r*
Percentage of housing units owner-occupied	.4924	.4924
Percentage with foreign-born parents	.5984	.1060
Age of city	.6223	.0239
Population density	.6344	.0121

Multiple *r* for 26 variables = .7300
R², corrected for degrees of freedom, = .48

TABLE A.16 *Public Housing Units per 1,000 Population*

Variable	Multiple *r*	Increase in *r*
Percentage of families below $3,000	.5543	.5543
Median school years completed	.6183	.0640
Percentage new to county since 1955	.6616	.0433
Percentage of housing units owner-occupied	.6790	.0174

Multiple *r* for 26 variables = .7061
R², corrected for degrees of freedom, = .44

TABLE A.17 *Per Capita Expenditures for Poverty Programs*

Variable	Multiple *r*	Increase in *r*
Age of city	.3707	.3707
Percentage of housing units owner-occupied	.4166	.0459
Total population	.4472	.0306
Percentage population change, 1950–1960	.4783	.0311
Age of population	.5011	.0228
Percentage foreign-born	.5433	.0422
Percentage of families below $3,000	.5614	.0181

Multiple *r* for 26 variables = .6097
R², corrected for degrees of freedom, = .30

Index